BROWN BELT
CROSSWORDS

EDITED BY RICH NORRIS

MARTIAL ARTS CROSSWORDS

HARD

PUZZLE
WRIGHT
PRESS

New York

**PUZZLE
WRIGHT
PRESS**

New York

An Imprint of Sterling Publishing
387 Park Avenue South
New York, NY 10016

PUZZLEWRIGHT PRESS and the distinctive Puzzlewright Press logo are
registered trademarks of Sterling Publishing Co., Inc.

The puzzles in this book were originally published in the Los Angeles Times from 2000 to 2002 and
appeared in the "Los Angeles Times Crosswords" series by Sterling Publishing Co., Inc.

ISBN 978-1-4549-1083-1

Distributed in Canada by Sterling Publishing
c/o Canadian Manda Group, 165 Dufferin Street
Toronto, Ontario, Canada M6K 3H6
Distributed in the United Kingdom by GMC Distribution Services
Castle Place, 166 High Street, Lewes, East Sussex, England BN7 1XU
Distributed in Australia by Capricorn Link (Australia) Pty. Ltd.
P.O. Box 704, Windsor, NSW 2756, Australia

For information about custom editions, special sales, and premium and corporate purchases,
please contact Sterling Special Sales at 800-805-5489 or specialsales@sterlingpublishing.com.

Manufactured in the United States of America

2   4   6   8   10   9   7   5   3   1

www.puzzlewright.com

CONTENTS

INTRODUCTION

Welcome to "Brown Belt Crosswords," the third in a four-book series designed to increase your crossword skills. If you like challenging crosswords, you are in for a real treat.

The 88 puzzles that follow first appeared on Fridays in the Los Angeles Times and were edited by crossword sensei Rich Norris. They've been selected for their clever themes and quality grids, and every clue has been calibrated to provide a substantial mental workout.

Once you've earned your brown belt in crosswords (by finishing every puzzle in this book), you'll be ready to continue your education by moving on to the next book in the series, "Black Belt Crosswords."

Happy solving!

1

by BILL ZAIS

ACROSS

1 Pet rocks and hula hoops
5 Kind of duck
9 Yawns
14 Dutch explorer Tasman
15 "More's the pity"
16 Take as one's own
17 Advice for those in line?
19 "Yikes!"
20 Try hard
21 Saloon serving
23 Jaworski's predecessor
24 Superman's X-ray vision?
28 Sports jacket feature
31 Sane
32 MPG rater
33 Expressed openly
38 "Okey-doke"
39 "___ the World Ends": 1975 hit
40 Reports on former spouses?
42 Golfer's concern
43 Char
45 Actress Bloom
46 Tolkien creature
47 Name names
49 Rob of "Melrose Place"
51 Golf fees?
54 Atlanta-based cable sta.
55 Man of many morals
56 Stat
60 Etching materials
63 Apiarist's favorite films?
65 Oft-dipped snack
66 Alternatively
67 Seth's son
68 Jordanian seaport
69 Transport using runners
70 Average

DOWN

1 Web info sources
2 Touch on
3 Roadside grazer
4 Regulated channel
5 Foam rubber component
6 Clay, now
7 Ornamental tree
8 Position paper
9 Village green structure
10 Lovers
11 Fighting word
12 Center opening?
13 Sault ___ Marie
18 Develop
22 Masculine, e.g.
25 Lucky charm
26 Iwo Jima figure
27 Hard rains
28 Allows access to
29 Per
30 Camelot sight
34 Shines
35 Giants' gp.

36 ___ Maria
37 New Haven student
41 Taken care of
44 Drum sound
48 Sonora snooze
50 Ranges
52 Hoop sites
53 Short time

54 Broken, in a way
57 El ___
58 Big execs
59 Old gas
60 Drillers' org.?
61 ___ au vin
62 Phrase with nutshell
64 Computer add-on

2

BY NELSON HARDY

ACROSS

1 One-third of Neapolitan, for short
5 Schlep
9 Mild epithet
14 Ex-"Tonight Show" host
15 Not bad
16 Greek fabulist
17 Type of sch.
18 Armistice exposé?
20 Defendant's dodge
22 Contaminates
23 Big sale at the art gallery?
25 Quick
29 Waffle expert?
30 Forcible ejection
31 Court VIPs
32 Actress MacDowell
35 Word in an ultimatum
36 Satellite with gardens?
39 Circus clapper
42 Mothers of Invention musician
43 Cabinet dept.
46 Argumentative
49 Prima ballerina
51 Tanner of tennis
52 Tear from a city slicker?
54 Wheat component
56 Prefix with Croatian
57 Horn player's asset?
61 Reptilian ending
62 Flight segment
63 Actor Morales
64 River residue
65 Slammer
66 Marvel Comics supergroup
67 Cool drinks

DOWN

1 Vacuumed and dusted
2 Extremely
3 Some Iroquois
4 Searched thoroughly
5 FDR's successor
6 Vital conduit
7 Order from a regular
8 Centers of activity
9 Calif. barrio city
10 Settles a score
11 Japanese volcano Mount ___
12 "Le Coq ___": Rimsky-Korsakov
13 Snoop
19 Suffix with differ
21 Exemplar
24 Rubik with a cube
26 M.p.h.
27 Questioning interjections
28 Wade opponent
30 Rope material
33 Nodding off

34 The Monkees' "___ Believer"
36 Formal
37 Newspaper page
38 Hall's singing partner
39 Abbr. on old maps
40 Author Umberto
41 "___ poetica": Horace work
43 Reason for a blackout, perhaps
44 Bead
45 Spreads the news

47 Frost lines?
48 She played Roz on "Frasier"
50 Texas city named by Russians
52 Ben Franklin's belief
53 Forearm bones
55 Ariz. neighbor
57 Cookbook abbr.
58 Siouan speaker
59 Furniture wood
60 Pink lady liquor

3

BY RICHARD HUGHES

ACROSS

1 Posthaste
5 Cut (down)
9 Praises
14 Heroes
15 Sign
16 Display to be proud of
17 Family record
18 Adriatic resort
19 Trite
20 Start of a quip
23 1950 suspense classic
24 Imitate
25 On the road
30 Stargazer's aid
35 Paul's "Exodus" role
36 Bedtime distraction
38 Phony beginning?
39 More of the quip
43 Wallet stuffers
44 "___ ride": gambler's order
45 Byron's "before"
46 Pater ___
49 Countenance
51 Furrow
53 Succeeded
54 End of the quip
63 Short shots
64 "___ me?"
65 "Venerable" saint
66 Pulitzer writer Dillard

67 Sister of Rachel
68 Lounge
69 Super Bowl I MVP
70 Eastern monk
71 River to Kassel, Germany

DOWN

1 City SE of Turin
2 It breaks at beaches
3 Genesis shepherd
4 False
5 Bohemian wedding activity
6 François's friend
7 Sly Foxx
8 ___ Gay
9 "A Hard Day's Night" director Richard
10 It may follow an overture
11 ___ Bator
12 Artist influenced by Freud
13 WWII weapon
21 Some Scandinavians
22 Suitable
25 Georgia city on the Ocmulgee
26 Maine college town
27 Does floor work
28 Carol
29 Heartache
31 Hosp. area
32 Cell predecessor
33 Earthy tone

34 Indulges, with "on"
37 Novel ending
40 Mil. carrier
41 Longfellow subject
42 Footballer Graham et al.
47 Schoolbag item
48 Capek play
50 Not equipped
52 Woven fabric

54 Yr.-end visitors
55 Reunion attendee
56 1992 erupter
57 Fuss
58 Sailing
59 "The King and I" setting
60 Its symbol is Pb
61 Cooper's tool
62 Bucks, e.g.

4

BY BILL ZAIS

ACROSS

1 Stimulate, as curiosity
6 Shaker formula
10 Blind alley site
14 Vent
15 Needle case
16 Predictor
17 Belt zone
18 Medieval meals?
20 Immobilizing device
22 Open-sided structures
23 Boy preceder
26 Chaps
28 "___ I Kissed You": Everly Brothers hit
29 Medieval devotee of body armor?
34 Equipped
35 Drop-off point
36 Tough guy
38 Penpoint
39 Not as vague
43 Bruin who wore #4
44 ___-American
46 Martinique, e.g.
47 Cumberland Gap explorer
49 Medieval history?
53 Pull
54 Minimal
55 Slaughter on the diamond
56 Beethoven's "Appassionata" et al.
60 Secure with lines
62 Medieval headgear?
64 Skagerrak feature
68 Cigar butt?
69 Call out to, perhaps
70 Port follower
71 Sorrows
72 Rooney of "60 Minutes"
73 Actor Max von ___

DOWN

1 Place of worship
2 "Deathtrap" playwright Levin
3 On the ___ vive: watchful
4 Not for the hoi polloi
5 Sundance's lover
6 Lipton competitor
7 Wore away
8 Crimp
9 "Television for women" network
10 Romantic, as an evening
11 Latin I word
12 Broadway's first Tevye
13 Loose ___
19 Conrad of "Diff'rent Strokes"
21 Librarian's warning
23 Range maker
24 Duty
25 Musical tone color
27 Dreamlike

30 Music store inventory
31 Pooh-bah
32 Certain victor
33 Face
37 Zane and Lady Jane
40 Grandson of Nokomis
41 Bar none
42 Baseball stat
45 Service interruptions
48 More than delight
50 Biblical verb
51 Knuckle under

52 Company requirement?
56 Bias
57 Not tricked by
58 Informal evening?
59 Diagnostic technique
61 Ices, so to speak
63 Band ending?
65 Passé
66 South American capital until 1960
67 Chemicals name

5

BY STEPHEN WINDHEIM

ACROSS
1 Gal Fri.
5 Teases
10 Repetitive process
14 Mrs. Yitzhak Rabin
15 Overhead
16 What this ans. is
17 Champion gofer?
19 Suffering sound
20 ___ Island
21 Pliers, e.g.
23 "Dancing Queen" group
25 Soft mineral
26 Pkg. delivery company
29 Forty-niner's score
31 Golden Horde member
35 Naval strength
38 Exile like Napoleon
39 Misogynist, for one
40 Tiny climber (removed to create this puzzle's theme entries)
42 Computer letters
43 Rare antelopes
45 Semisweet white wine
47 Milk curdling agent
48 "___ the season ..."
49 All arranged
50 Barney's pal
52 Magnifying device
55 Certified
59 Small dressing table

63 Film noir knife
64 Ernie's Russian cousin?
66 Window section
67 Circular sandwiches
68 Roll and bind, as a sail
69 Night light
70 Small amphibians
71 Durable wood

DOWN
1 Sight from Salzburg
2 Senate unit
3 It's a long story
4 Eighth Greek letter
5 Path to the gold, so they say
6 Son of, in Arabic names
7 Bell sound
8 Six-time U.S. Open champ
9 Arranged in rows
10 Walkway holdup?
11 Heckelphone relative
12 Skier's aid
13 Sea eagles
18 Part of WWW
22 Mercury, for one
24 Math calculation
26 Theater guide
27 "Positive thinking" advocate
28 Old Nick
30 Dadaist Max
32 Peter and Paul
33 Skirt style
34 Sublease

14

36 Reaction from Sean's fan club?

37 Directions

41 A suspect might have one

44 Texas topper

46 Having no point

51 Big name in farm equipment

53 San Francisco's ___ Hill

54 Fictional inventor Tom

55 African cobras

56 Which

57 Singer Turner

58 Took a lot?

60 Dejected

61 Gumbo pod

62 Egg segment

65 Grasped

6

BY ROBERT H. WOLFE

ACROSS

1 Line of cliffs
6 Comedian Mort
10 With 26-Across, command at a cave door
14 More fit
15 Nautical direction
16 Remain
17 Miss by ___
18 Queen of the Olympian gods
19 Swan lover of myth
20 Old wharf assessments?
22 Exam type
23 Tap dancer Powell
24 Suspend
26 See 10-Across
29 Plumed heron
32 Some church officials
35 Extra stipulations
37 Emotional poem
38 Frame of mind
39 Wax theatrical
41 Court action
42 Buddy
43 Peter, for one
44 Experts
46 It's commonly twisted
48 Chain of hills
50 1960 Summer Olympics site
52 Temporary substitute

56 ___ motion
58 Wharf parking area?
61 Diner employee
62 Eligible, to the SSS
63 Native of Israel
64 High spot
65 Dostoevsky's denial
66 Bay
67 Looking up
68 Big name in locks
69 Indigent

DOWN

1 Stratified rock
2 Desert carrier
3 Animated
4 Allowed to go
5 Peacock, e.g.
6 "The English Patient" setting
7 "Roots" author Haley
8 "Looky ___!"
9 Boxer restraint
10 Like a pool table's shape
11 Wharf organization?
12 Icelandic epic
13 Actress Patricia
21 Flips
25 DDE's opponent
27 New Zealand native
28 Ending with differ
30 Work for People, perhaps
31 Asian holidays
32 Actress Thompson

33 Shark's offer
34 Wharf storage facilities?
36 Scarcity
40 Bell and others
41 Pontooned flier
43 Pro ___
45 Visits unexpectedly
47 Subtle
49 Extensive property

51 Ethnic magazine since 1945
53 Gothic architecture feature
54 Landed
55 Like some moss
56 Sign of a fight?
57 Nuts
59 Irish singer/songwriter
60 Film unit

7

BY DIANE EPPERSON

ACROSS
1 Juno's Greek counterpart
5 Pelvic bones
10 Blowout
14 Yaks in yokes
15 Without a guide
16 Busy as ___
17 C to C, e.g.
19 Boris Godunov, for one
20 Immortal Kentucky coach Rupp
21 Dark principle
22 Cut
23 Glue, e.g.
24 Unburden
26 Julio Gallo, e.g.
29 Linda of "Jekyll & Hyde"
31 Conciliatory bribe
33 ___ space
34 "Battlestar Galactica" commander
36 Puts in but good
37 Reflection
39 Retro dresses
41 Blue Grotto locale
42 Tuscany marble-exporting city
43 Type of dancer
44 Depilatory cream

48 Australian Outback dweller
50 Former Bruin great
52 HST's successor
53 Local mail ctr.
54 Hit hard
56 Head honcho
58 Expression of relief
59 Expansive western U.S. desert region
61 Essen pronoun
62 Sound introduction?
63 Climactic passage
64 ___'acte
65 Chelmsford's county
66 Organic compound

DOWN
1 Reverence
2 Displayed in abundance
3 Do a shoemaker's job
4 Indigo-yielding shrub
5 Trendy eateries
6 Mandela's org.
7 Pottery medium
8 Go through again
9 Certain Yemeni
10 Prohibition product
11 Type of landlord
12 Agar source
13 "And I Love ___": Beatles
18 EMT's skill
25 Major-___: steward
27 Garciaparra of baseball

18

28 B&O et al.
30 Cloudburst
32 Stash finder
35 Hope
36 Customs duty
37 Wasted, as youth
38 Shakespearean villain
39 UN delegate
40 "Sock it to me!" show, familiarly
43 Distorts

45 Expands one's home
46 1966 Mary Martin musical
47 Kingly
49 Plead, as a case
51 Deprive
55 1986 World Series winners
57 Speed
58 Minute
60 Modern art?

8

BY DAVID J. KAHN

ACROSS

1 Nebraska's largest city
6 See eye to eye
10 Night fliers
14 About half of Israel
15 Bailiwick
16 Perlman of "Cheers"
17 League of Women Voters founder
19 That's an order
20 Colorado native
21 Lots
22 Maryland athlete, briefly
23 ___ shadow
24 "This Boy's Life" memoirist
28 Camera attachment
29 French pronoun
30 "___ we there yet?"
31 Pique
33 Buyer's consideration
34 Captured
35 College football coach for 71 years
40 "___ folly to be wise": Gray
41 Undecided
42 Words of assent: Var.
43 "___ a living"
44 Notable period
45 Certain agts.

48 Notorious pirate
51 Relative of -like
54 School period
55 Author Kingsley
56 Whopper
57 Fresh
58 He hit 58 homers in 1932
61 Come up suddenly
62 Chick's tail?
63 Flood restraint
64 Pot part
65 Prohibitions
66 Wooden Mortimer

DOWN

1 When prompted
2 Substantial
3 See eye to eye
4 LBJ beagle
5 Fly
6 "The Monkey's Paw" author
7 Teheran resident
8 Risk
9 Consume
10 Gluck opera "___ ed Euridice"
11 1941 Triple Crown horse
12 Jumps by taking turns
13 Watched Junior
18 Harrow rival
22 Bothersome types
25 From ___: everything
26 Fair

27 ___ shui: architectural art
28 Former Secretary of Defense Aspin
31 Fake
32 Reform Party founder
33 MSNBC competitor
35 Ending for idiom
36 First-stringers
37 Actress Loughlin
38 Algerian port
39 Sunbather's goal
45 Tap-ins, in golf

46 Early 16th-century date
47 '50s flops
49 "I'm all ears"
50 Milt of "Pantomime Quiz"
51 "___ a Parade"
52 Philly player
53 Put a spell on
57 Menu phrase
58 Quick punch
59 Rhoda's mom
60 Marsh

9

BY MANNY NOSOWSKY

ACROSS

1 Bills
6 Campus military gp.
10 Indulgent
14 Pianist Claudio
15 Way off
16 "Ooh ___!"
17 Traveler's appliance?
20 PC "Get me out of here" key
21 Simple homes
22 Oft-photographed event
23 Russian beer
25 Verbal nudge
26 Finally
28 Rugby resident
29 Question of identity
32 Loud, sustained sound
33 Projected presentation
35 Bar menu suggestion?
38 Kid's hideout
39 "Got two fives for ___?"
40 Part of a crew
41 Got going
42 Like Disney's "Pinocchio," say
44 Newspaper department
45 Agree to more issues
46 Like magic
49 Signify
50 Balkan republic: Abbr.
53 Soprano's coach?
56 Whit or bit
57 Star followers
58 Competition site
59 On ___: without a firm buyer
60 Thornfield Hall governess
61 Songlike

DOWN

1 See
2 Makes a mistake
3 Building trades worker
4 Water source
5 Like
6 Large quantities
7 Does in
8 ___ kwon do
9 Troilus's love
10 Bias
11 Annual Epsom Downs race, with "the"
12 Get away fast
13 Piquant
18 Eject
19 Gather
24 Escape mechanism
25 Heyday
26 "I shall not find myself so ___ die": Brutus
27 Land
28 Great party, slangily
29 Starr concern
30 Got an edge on
31 Due (to)
33 Stinker

34 Say
36 [Sigh!]
37 Serves a sentence
42 Bring up
43 Marigold, for one
44 Fond ___, Wisconsin
45 Secure again
46 Actress Cornelia ___ Skinner

47 Cut short
48 Give credit to
49 Roman Cath. honorific
51 Actress Anderson
52 Bric-a-___
54 Thumbs-down
55 Have a bawl

10

BY NICK GRIVAS

ACROSS
1 Test sites
5 Bugs of the underworld
10 Market opening?
14 Concerning
15 Muse with a lyre
16 Surfer, perhaps
17 "Good grief!"
18 "Rich Man, Poor Man" actor
19 "The Little Red Hen" response
20 Yvonne's favorite don?
23 1985 Kate Nelligan film
24 Red Guard idol
25 Young newt
27 Singer Stewart
28 Shout
32 "We ___ please"
34 Black Sea country
37 Bryn ___
38 Hugh's favorite skater?
41 Tucked in
42 Spanish sheep
43 Lots of plots
45 Carpet layer's calculation
46 West of "Klondike Annie"
49 Dawson of the NFL
50 "___ Buttermilk Sky"
53 Oodles

55 Jeanette's favorite financier?
60 Wanderer
61 Ellington contemporary
62 Eastern leader
63 Alice's immortalizer
64 Humpback habitat
65 Draped garment
66 Cad
67 Opening
68 Tallow source

DOWN
1 Schubert songs
2 "Measure for Measure" deputy
3 Prepared, as for a jolt
4 Accord or Camry
5 Ground grain
6 Roughly
7 Pealed
8 Top players
9 Bellini opera
10 1936 Pasteur portrayer
11 Unanimously
12 Pair
13 ___ Lanka
21 TV host Lake
22 Feathery stole
26 Rocky pinnacle
29 Saroyan's "My Name Is ___"
30 Runner's assignment
31 Sign of autumn
33 "___ corny ...": song lyric

34 Impulse
35 Roulette bet
36 Aachen article
38 Again
39 Combustible
40 It may precede a shot
41 Actor Mineo
44 Grass transplant
46 '50s Kenyan revolutionary

47 Venerate
48 Quickness of mind
51 Gray wolves
52 Pass
54 Pungent green
56 Deliberate
57 Between ports
58 Make-up artist?
59 Impression
60 "A likely story!"

11

BY DAVID J. KAHN

ACROSS

1 Take ___ view of
5 Musical with the song "Memory"
9 Bubbling
14 Taboo
15 Mohammad Khan, for one
16 One of the Marxes
17 Steve McQueen's last film
19 17-Across, astronomically
20 Chill (out)
21 Skeptic's comment
23 Grace Kelly's last film
26 Pop
27 "Wheel of Fortune" request
28 Keep from practicing?
32 Capone's nemeses
33 Radiation unit
34 "Exodus" role
35 Frat badges
36 James Dean's last film
39 Wilbur Post's horse
40 Agcy. established under HST
41 Trouble
42 Caen's river
43 War ender
47 Early second-century date
48 Tailor's concern
49 Vivien Leigh's last film
52 Record album status
55 Hockey legend
56 Film with a stage?
57 John Belushi's last film
62 Shot at the bar
63 "___ Heartache": Tyler hit
64 1997 Peter Fonda role
65 Funny Youngman
66 Tennis stroke
67 Blind piece

DOWN

1 Worker on a farm
2 Play-___: modeling compound
3 Noticeable
4 Uncas's tribe
5 Fire
6 Ten percenter: Abbr.
7 Fredric March's last film
8 New York restaurateur
9 Rabbitlike rodent
10 Faddish animatronic "pets"
11 Fail to mention
12 To me, to Mimi
13 ___ Blanc
18 "That's awful"
22 Big ref. book
23 More comfy

24 Puppeteer Tony
25 "That's ___ haven't heard"
26 Mar. honoree
29 Aviator's maneuver
30 Contest sites
31 Jockey
37 Ingenuous one
38 "Finally, the weekend!"
39 Double-decker, for one
44 Not ahead

45 "___ days hath ..."
46 Negative truth
50 ___ Wars
51 29-Down response
52 Top-drawer
53 Strike zone?
54 Plenty
58 Bar opener
59 Breach
60 Actor Stephen
61 Kind of designer

12

BY ALFIO MICCI

ACROSS

1 Galileo's birthplace
5 Pile by a pitchfork
8 Reasonable
12 Over
13 River through Congo
14 Boundary
15 Artificial benefactor?
18 Go astray
19 "Horrors!"
20 Isaac's eldest
21 Rose oils
23 Bk. after Ezra
24 Cool type?
27 God with a hammer
28 Artificial pudding flavor?
32 Portage burdens
34 Bout site
35 "___ luego"
38 Skill
39 Fare
40 Out of bed
41 Harangue
43 Artificial Hawaii landmark?
45 Slangy turndown
49 Ethyl ending
50 Once called
51 Peddle
53 Red letters?
55 Go under
57 Stephen of "In Dreams"
58 Artificial luau garb?
61 Transferred employee's concern, briefly
62 Cut out
63 Suffix with confer
64 Walk with effort
65 Join
66 Like much fine wine

DOWN

1 Volkswagen family car
2 Tied to
3 Taken care of
4 Stun
5 Beatles film
6 Tissue ingredient
7 Evergreen with elastic wood
8 Vocabulary study aid
9 Cairo debut of 1871
10 Drafted
11 Spanish king
13 Perfect agreement
16 Scandinavian god of war
17 Sandra and Ruby
22 Frigid
23 Cosa ___
25 Teen troubler
26 Whaler's direction
29 Not fancy in the least
30 Bizarre
31 Get the bearings of
33 Tall, Biblically named plant
35 Skyline obscurer

36 A ___ apple
37 Crumby topping
42 Becalmed
44 Pianist Peter
46 Regatta activity
47 Gadsden Purchase president
48 On cloud nine

52 Trains overhead
54 Normandy battle town
55 Emit smoke
56 Desertlike
58 Dadaist Hans
59 Auto club service
60 Mauna ___

13

BY NICK GRIVAS

ACROSS

1 "... sting like ___": Ali
5 Harsh sound
9 Started
14 Shiloh locale: Abbr.
15 1952 Winter Olympics site
16 Bring forth
17 Lie (around)
18 Car roof with removable panels
19 Get hoodwinked
20 Start of a quip
23 Simple guy
24 Mouth, slangily
25 DLX ÷ X
28 Shirt with artwork, maybe
29 Oxford's river
33 Sans opposite
34 "Cheers" waitress
35 Court assistant
36 Quip, part 2
41 "There's a chance"
42 Shire of "Rocky"
43 Unveils, poetically
44 "Right away"
46 RR stop
49 Wide divergence
50 Lance of the bench
51 Driver's invitation
53 End of the quip

58 Let loose
60 Layered snack
61 Kansas playwight
62 Much-visited place
63 Cornell football rival
64 Poker bet
65 Is sore
66 90° from norte
67 Zeno of ___

DOWN

1 Finally
2 Campus topper
3 Organic catalyst
4 Año starter
5 Univ. recruiter
6 Italian wine region
7 Splash
8 Segar's sailor
9 Charlie Parker's genre
10 Constantly
11 Share equally
12 Police blotter entry
13 "Waking ___ Devine": 1998 film
21 Bait
22 Scale notes
26 Miles of movies
27 Revolting
30 "I told you!"
31 Part of Q and A: Abbr.
32 Israel Philharmonic director
33 "What Women Want" actor

34 "Unionism and Socialism" author Eugene

35 Bromide

36 Feature of a bad air day

37 Literary sobriquet

38 Pirate costume accessory

39 Western treaty gp.

40 Glob add-on

44 "___ your life"

45 Pessimist's phrase

46 ___ cord

47 Prickly sensation

48 Actress Bassett

50 "Don't get any ___"

52 Virtually assured

54 Cut up

55 Tram loads

56 Pay for a pad

57 Hue

58 Patrick's "Robin Hood" costar

59 Japanese computer giant

14

BY RICHARD HUGHES

ACROSS

1 Cleansing aid
5 "Les Misérables" inspector
11 ___ pro nobis
14 Coffee holders
15 Eastern Christian
16 Place
17 Start of a quip
19 Novel ending?
20 "Raindrops" singer Clark
21 Steel plow developer
22 Lariat
24 ___ Maria
25 Means to an end
26 Quip, part 2
32 "Middlemarch" author
33 Remove totally
34 Bound
35 Smeltery waste
36 Mass apparel
39 Put up
40 Copland ballet
42 Quip, part 3
47 Register
48 Simple card game
49 Tag
50 Big name in insurance
53 Good place to fight a losing battle?
56 Tour sponsor: Abbr.
57 End of the quip
60 Poetic contraction
61 1939 Giraudoux play
62 Southern bread
63 Dr. of rap
64 Hound
65 Prom attendee

DOWN

1 Part of QED
2 Faithful
3 Regarding, to attorneys
4 They may follow signatures: Abbr.
5 U.S. capital closest to Canada
6 Actress Bancroft
7 Competitor
8 Roof overhang
9 AAA suggestion
10 Luxury apartment feature
11 Pain-relieving drug
12 Bumpkin
13 Act offensively
18 Pindar, for one
23 "___ bin ein Berliner"
24 Ref's decision
25 Alec D'Urberville's slayer
26 Sunday seat
27 Quebec's ___ d'Orléans
28 El ___
29 Risk
30 Fishing lure
31 Foolhardy

35 Like some controls
36 Dog-days drink
37 Permit
38 Word before a scream, maybe
39 Dolly pusher
40 Charged
41 Lacto-___-vegetarian
42 Cried out
43 Medieval catapult
44 Suave

45 Fish eggs
46 Safari figure
50 Afterthoughts
51 Work on proofs
52 Sharp part
53 Do a blacksmith's job
54 Yearn
55 "So be it"
58 Suffix with prop or meth
59 Pull (out)

15

BY NICK GRIVAS

ACROSS
1 All-out
6 Cognac bottle letters
10 Hamlet, for one
14 Play a card?
15 Without peers
16 Transport to Tel Aviv
17 Apt author of "Instant Wealth for Dummies"?
19 Agra attire
20 Rhymed works
21 White House feature
23 City west of Tulsa
25 Artist Max
26 Apt author of "Continental Breakfast for Dummies"?
32 Put on a pedestal
33 Game with pitching
34 Intimidate
37 Outdo
38 New Artist Grammy winner of 1990
40 So
41 Army member
42 Clark's "Betrayed" costar
43 Luigi's love
44 Apt author of "Astrology for Dummies"?
47 Auto option, e.g.
50 Corp. bigwig
51 Hawaii's largest industry
54 Oft-censored works
59 Vigorous style
60 Apt author of "Carpeting for Dummies"?
62 Pimples on pupils
63 Nice notion
64 Find, as facts
65 Track event
66 Neutral, for one
67 Highbrows

DOWN
1 Diamond cover
2 "Typee" sequel
3 Cream holder
4 Flea market warning
5 Easy
6 Pickle company with a spokesstork
7 Trinity member
8 Doing mil. drudge work, maybe
9 Monterrey money
10 Stewart title role
11 Actor Delon
12 They make busts
13 "Four Quartets" poet
18 Yield
22 Ocean danger
24 Greyhound event
26 First name in country
27 Team members
28 After everyone else

29 Supermodel Carol
30 Adversary
31 Take wing
34 Come (up)
35 Meany
36 Trials
38 Word with pool or wash
39 Literary collection
40 Funny Philips
42 Actress Anderson
43 Reconciliations
44 Dangerous stinger
45 New England prep
   school town

46 Parched
47 First string
48 "La ___ Vita"
49 Rock and Roll Hall
   of Famer Eddy
52 More than a sip
53 Created
55 Certain bed
56 "O, beware, my lord,
   of jealousy" speaker
57 Group with
   members
58 Swiss ___
61 Country expanse

16

BY GREG STAPLES

ACROSS

1 Freshness
5 "I ___ my wit's end"
9 Bailiwicks
14 Jai ___
15 Fasten, in a way
16 Round numbers
17 Master scheduler?
20 Pad holder
21 Stint
22 Prepare for a snap
24 Chairs' lists
28 Chemical fig.
31 "Shake ___!"
33 Type of sock
34 Like schlock
36 St. Petersburg's river
39 "AbFab" producer
40 Bean Town slowpoke?
43 "___ for Evidence"
44 One on the move
45 "Golf for Women"
   author Suggs
46 Slant unfairly
48 Sort
50 Smithsonian, for one:
   Abbr.
51 Duties
54 English school since
   1440
56 Combustion engine
   pioneer
58 Catching device
62 Walk like Santa?
66 Row of pawns, e.g.
67 "Very interesting"
68 None too happy
69 Saw things?
70 Wee-hours
71 Dog follower

DOWN

1 Fifth Avenue retailer
2 Touched down
3 Lucid
4 Roadside aid
5 229-year-old TV alien
6 Barbie's maker
7 Yearn
8 "Dawson's Creek" extra
9 Clear blue
10 Temporary ruler
11 Energy amount
12 Web giant, briefly
13 Vane dir.
18 Game winner
19 Wine holder
23 Refuse
25 Sean O'Casey's
   birthplace
26 Mother superior
27 Whispered item
28 In ideal circumstances
29 Three-horse carriage
30 Suez Crisis
   precipitator
32 Contest submission
35 Not share

37 Hotel employee
38 Before now
41 Shoves off
42 "The Bridge on the River Kwai" Oscar winner
47 Doohickey
49 Bit of buckshot
52 Serious grime
53 Charge

55 ___Kosh B'Gosh: kids' clothing line
57 Socialite Maxwell
59 Military no-show
60 Unusual
61 Checked out
62 Scribble
63 Yegg's diamond
64 Former comm. giant
65 Place to start a hole

17

BY S.I. MURPHY II

ACROSS
1 Switch on a radio
5 Fancy timepiece
10 Dweeb
14 "Star Wars" princess
15 Afghan's neighbor
16 Sigmund's daughter
17 ___ scout
18 Place to watch animals gamble?
20 Carpeting calculation
21 Transvaal native
22 Bagel flavoring
23 Bond opponent
25 Russian grassland
26 Kennel measuring device?
31 Foreigner
32 Those with
33 Hope in Hollywood
36 Be dependent
37 Value
38 Over
39 ___ canto
40 Info-gathering exchange
41 Explorer ___ de León
42 Designated area for ram disputes?
44 Financially solvent
47 Not of the cloth
48 Radar images

49 Cinema canine
52 Fake
55 Turkey in traffic?
57 Met star
58 Italy's Villa d'___
59 Concert cry
60 By and by
61 In heels, say
62 Hoopster
63 Look bored, in a way

DOWN
1 Seaweed, e.g.
2 Golda of Israel
3 School exercise
4 Hogwash
5 Military decoration
6 Two-toned treat
7 Running behind
8 ___'acte
9 Sundial number
10 "Siegfried" composer
11 Remove a coat lining, perhaps
12 Get nosy
13 River to the Rhone
19 They're taken in class
24 "Collages" novelist Anaïs
25 Leave in
26 Fishhook feature
27 Nautical direction
28 1814 treaty site
29 ___ Gras
30 Perrier alternative
33 Fancy setting

34 In the old days
35 Carole King's "___ to Canaan"
37 Savannah's "Today" cohost
38 "The Pajama Game" star
40 Seeming
41 Couples's gp.
42 Hit
43 Allure

44 French clerics
45 Blood partner
46 Be false with
49 Tourist city east of Jaipur
50 Antlered animal
51 "Slithy" thing
53 Declare openly
54 "The Magic Mountain" author
56 "Friends" network

18

BY PRAVEEN GODAY

ACROSS
1 Imitates
5 Buck of filmdom
10 Swine swill
14 Class ender
15 Genius
16 Own
17 A son of Isaac
18 Men with polish
19 Church chorus
20 Barcelona buccaneer?
23 Devotees
24 Make out
25 "60 Minutes" correspondent
28 Strongholds
33 WWW addresses
34 Stock marketeer
36 Court divider
37 1941 Milanese movie classic?
40 French article
41 Familiarize with new material
42 Make an impression
43 Unmistakably
45 Sidekicks
46 Spanish king
47 Regarding
49 Bordeaux breakup?
56 Soup vegetables
57 ___ vincit amor
58 Foretell
59 Otherwise
60 Pool
61 Sign
62 Jetty
63 Inventor Howe
64 Alien: Prefix

DOWN
1 Explorer Tasman
2 Cozumel currency
3 Fire
4 High-scoring game
5 Small shot shooter
6 Fields of study
7 Jazz flutist Herbie
8 Partners of pieces
9 Assertive
10 Cut close
11 Shiny fabric
12 More than
13 Quill, once
21 Unsettle
22 Find out
25 Present tersely
26 Circus Maximus, for one
27 Fast
28 Partridge flock
29 Nobelist Pavlov
30 Finished
31 Sierra ___
32 Puts back in
34 Bit of locker room humor
35 Stir up

38 Hopeless case
39 Couch potato's fixation
44 Rubber
45 Put away
47 Screenwriter Loos
48 Does in
49 Supermarket counter

50 Lessen
51 Czech Olympian Zatopek
52 Not behind
53 Big volume
54 Paradise
55 City on the Truckee
56 Pizazz

19

BY MARY ANN DEES

ACROSS

1 Starbucks order
6 Priests' garb
10 Bartok and Gabor
14 Kharg Island resident
15 In ___ of
16 Stash finder
17 Disgusting office supply?
19 Island south of Florida
20 Ran into
21 Risqué
23 Has a grand old time
27 1964 Nobel Prize decliner
28 Hill components?
29 ___ lane: carpooler's access
32 TKO caller
33 To be, in old Rome
34 Not fooled by
36 Moderating suffix
39 Nonsense
40 Movers' association?
41 St. Louis-to-Chicago dir.
42 Coppertone tube abbr.
43 Whole
44 Purim's month
45 Toronto's prov.

47 1967 NHL Rookie of the Year
48 Sharp
49 Racket
52 Hospital employee
54 Revitalizing force
57 Orion's lover, in myth
58 False idol
59 Time at which speech begins?
64 160 square rods
65 Genesis grandchild
66 Gang lands
67 Ruby and garnet
68 Position
69 Follow carefully

DOWN

1 Stk. payment
2 "___ tu": Verdi aria
3 White House nickname
4 Windflower
5 Military band members
6 Each
7 Resort on the lagoon of Venice
8 Complaint
9 Wanders through cyberspace
10 Ovation follower, at times
11 Tunneling bank robber?
12 Shady spot
13 Alarm
18 Polo Grounds great
22 Chocolate substitute

23 "Ten code" talkers
24 Noted moralist
25 Immense cager?
26 Eastern faith
30 Dorian's creator
31 Shoelaces alternative
34 Pale
35 King whose tomb was found in 1922
37 Pound sound
38 Like some marinades
40 Necessary
44 Defrauds (of), slangily
46 Dukes, say
48 Votes to accept
49 Open, in a way
50 ___ Corps
51 Stereotypical dog name
53 Fam. member
55 O'Neill's daughter
56 Raid competitor
60 "Don't ___!"
61 Chemist Remsen
62 Saints' gp.
63 Sympathetic utterance

20

BY RANDALL J. HARTMAN

ACROSS

1 Happy, to José
6 Raises, perhaps
10 Take off
14 Ticked off
15 Immediately after
16 Kyrgyzstan's ___ Mountains
17 Matter of fact
18 ___ majesty
19 Fatigue
20 Procession for Saint-Saëns?
23 Pipe part
24 Dossier letters
25 Byrnes of "77 Sunset Strip"
26 Prohibit
29 Dance, slangily
31 ___-Cat
33 Met moment
35 ___ me tangere: touch-me-not
37 Duplicate
41 Offenbach testifying?
44 Near
45 Sicilian resort
46 Rig on the road
47 "I get it!"
49 Dealer's tip, in slang
51 So far

52 One who makes calls at home
55 Two-time U.S. Open champ
57 Penny
59 Demands from Boulez?
64 Mitchell plantation
65 Check
66 Horseshoe-shaped hardware item
68 Skip
69 Soothing application
70 Listening device
71 Aswan's river
72 ___-Ball
73 Type of test

DOWN

1 ___ leaf
2 Guitarist Clapton
3 Etna output
4 Tabloid features
5 Top
6 1912 Progressive Party member
7 Olympics event
8 Maria Callas role
9 Slinks
10 Numbers, maybe
11 Oil source
12 Electrical measure
13 Diabolical type
21 Italian director Sergio
22 "Bonanza" setting
26 Gulf of California peninsula

27 Kuwaiti, e.g.
28 Petrocelli of '60s-'70s baseball
30 Ignition aid
32 Corrida cheers
34 Water color
36 Clean hands, so to speak
38 Follow the rules
39 Bering Sea city
40 Lit sign
42 King Arthur's father
43 Grabs

48 APBs, say
50 Guarantee
52 Author Sinclair
53 "___ Vice"
54 Hazard
56 Use the pulpit
58 Marching band members
60 Assess
61 Stir up
62 Wands
63 Director Kazan
67 Christmas list item

21

BY LILA CHERRY

ACROSS

1 Please
8 Pastoral poem
15 Separating devices
16 Loafers, e.g.
17 Election hopeful
18 Try to keep quiet
19 HOOK
21 Spotted
22 Tram filler
23 Café lightener
26 Hula ___
28 Univ. hotshots
33 Former "Tonight Show" announcer Hall
34 Blacken
35 Sheep trills
36 LINE
39 Kind of truth
40 Greenspan's concern: Abbr.
41 "I'm in favor!"
42 Days of Hanukkah, say
43 Admit
44 Bk. before Job
45 Mid-11th-century date
46 Roman goddess of peace
48 SINKER
55 Nannies
56 Conceived beforehand
59 One on a board
60 Serf
61 Most acidic
62 Malign

DOWN

1 IRS Form 1040 datum
2 G.I. address
3 Pat down
4 Most distant
5 Actress Berger
6 Act the gadabout
7 River through Belgium
8 Steep slope
9 Ripoff
10 Shown while happening
11 Candid
12 Cheney's predecessor
13 E pluribus ___
14 Behold
20 Unfortunate type
23 Lay off
24 Type of committee
25 That is, in Latin
27 It may be in a lock
28 "Mission: Impossible" actress
29 American Airlines Center player, for short
30 Is law-abiding
31 Insertion symbol
32 Checkup request
34 Cancel a dele
35 Air-concentrating tubes
37 Take after
38 Prefix with system
43 Prepared
44 Commodities tax

46

45 Stallions' mates
47 "It's ___!": warning shout
48 ___ not incl.: product caveat
49 Saintly glow
50 Incite
51 Right on a map
52 Mouthful
53 One of a '60s pop quartet
54 Icy coating
57 ER workers
58 Brooklyn add-on

<table>
<tr><td>1</td><td>2</td><td>3</td><td>4</td><td>5</td><td>6</td><td>7</td><td></td><td>8</td><td>9</td><td>10</td><td>11</td><td>12</td><td>13</td><td>14</td></tr>
<tr><td>15</td><td></td><td></td><td></td><td></td><td></td><td></td><td></td><td>16</td><td></td><td></td><td></td><td></td><td></td><td></td></tr>
<tr><td>17</td><td></td><td></td><td></td><td></td><td></td><td></td><td></td><td>18</td><td></td><td></td><td></td><td></td><td></td><td></td></tr>
</table>

22

BY ANNE GARELLICK

ACROSS

1 1975 Wimbledon champ
5 Flies
9 Waste, as time
13 Deceptive type
14 Perfect
16 Car bar
17 ___ many words
18 With 63-Across, signmaker of this puzzle
19 Fervor
20 Jingle on an old sign, part 1
23 Farm follower?
24 Bring home pizza, e.g.
25 Teeth site
28 Choice parts
32 Stand waiter
35 Jingle, part 2
39 Experts
41 Jazz singer O'Day
42 Formal opening?
43 Jingle, part 3
46 Religious sch.
47 Andalucía address
48 Stingers
50 Anjous
54 Great
58 End of jingle
62 One on the other side
63 See 18-Across

64 Son of Jacob
65 Buck
66 Some are tall
67 Uniform
68 Year-end party favor
69 Curved
70 Actress Harper

DOWN

1 Pulitzer winner Walker
2 Biblical mount
3 Urgency
4 Steamy
5 Sailing maneuver
6 Pt. of HEW
7 ___ verte: green earth
8 South Pacific tourist stop
9 Sloth
10 Plow pullers
11 Blast furnace residue
12 Moray
15 Go on
21 Rise impressively
22 Farm feature
26 Diner offering
27 Marching group
29 Porters
30 Georgia ___: Atlanta stadium
31 Sink alternative
32 Broadway's Grizabella and Macavity
33 Flu symptom
34 Pod resident
36 Beak

37 Leftover piece
38 Big blow
40 Light alternative
44 Black-and-white bite
45 Not as much
49 Renter's rental
51 Netherlands cap.
52 Restorative program, briefly
53 Gain or loss indicator

55 Annoyance
56 Overhanging edges
57 Greek tourist attractions
58 A big fan of
59 Distinguished
60 Inferno
61 "The Day of the Locust" author
62 Campfire residue

23

BY DAVID J. KAHN

ACROSS
1 Jr.'s concern
5 Excited state
9 Be ready for
14 Heaps
15 Daughter of Zeus
16 Ezio Pinza, for one
17 Te-heed
19 Taking after
20 Start of a very short joke
22 Genetic "messenger"
23 "___ Kapital"
24 Pick up
25 Kett of old comics
27 Joke, part 2
30 "___ a traveler ...":
Shelley
34 Activists
36 Bank's protection
38 Old greeting
39 Joke, part 3
43 Zilch
44 Make ___ for it
45 Saw opening?
46 Trifles
48 Joke, part 4
50 Bonkers
51 Where-at link
53 Abu Dhabi is its cap.
56 Coll. hopefuls
57 End of the joke
63 Kind of rules

64 Neither here nor there
66 Upholstery braid
67 Laundry emanation
68 Ballerina Pavlova
69 Bar Harbor locale
70 Dope
71 Unspecified ones

DOWN
1 Some govt. heads
2 Fort Sam Houston site
3 With spirit
4 Tickle Me Elmo maker
5 "___ Lady": Tom Jones
song
6 Mother of note
7 "___ to differ"
8 Start from scratch
9 Dishonor
10 Rockies denizen
11 Exemplary phrase
12 "Money ___ everything"
13 Diner request
18 Put on the canvas
21 Everglades wader
22 Patio crawler
26 Oils and such
28 Emotionless, as a look
29 Quality
31 Fussed publicly
32 Laurels, e.g.
33 Lands, in Livorno
35 ___ Na Na
37 Catcher
40 Rub off
41 "Speed" speeder

42 Eggy concoction
47 Observes, with "on"
49 Waterfall phenomenon
52 The ones here
54 Golden finish?
55 Pond breeder
57 Word in a letter
opening

58 Lively dance
59 Cosmonaut
Gagarin
60 Oz visitor
61 French wave
62 "O! what ___
of looks ...": Shak.
65 Writer Hentoff

24

BY David Covill

ACROSS
1 "The Fortune Cookie" Oscar winner
8 Masters
14 Passionate
15 Byzantine treasures
17 Becoming less important
19 Old Queens stadium
20 It might get a boost
21 S, in communications
22 Fun house sound
25 Shuffle
26 Rodeo gear
29 Winged god
31 Prank
32 Cabbage with curled leaves
34 Second-largest Atlantic coast city
37 Punching out
41 "Ulalume" monogram
42 Cutting
43 Effort
44 Solicitation
46 Capital in Lewis and Clark County
47 Gothic adornment
50 Defendant, often
53 Disquiet
55 Rocker's job
56 Pac-12 sports powerhouse
60 Shining unexpectedly
63 Stretchable
64 Fix, as a basket
65 Bob of oaters
66 Agamemnon's son

DOWN
1 Gym supplies
2 Eastern nurse
3 Vegas tip
4 Early dinosaur period
5 Doll
6 Boring tools
7 Treatment
8 Anti-smoking org.
9 8-Down members
10 Greenland native
11 Tree-lined streets, in Tijuana
12 Park levels
13 Spook
16 Mast support
18 Python, for one
23 Get ready to fire
24 Dieter's breakfast
26 Vacation spot
27 O'Neill's "___ Christie"
28 Where to get off
30 Ump's kin
32 Massage
33 Mature
34 Father Time's garb
35 Pressing need
36 Cajun vegetable

38 Clanton gang leader
39 Escape
40 Tusked mammals
44 "Say ___"
45 Actress Caron
46 More expensive
47 Vane mover
48 Builds a pot
49 Sports commentator Musberger

51 Breakfast staple
52 Part of TNT
54 Cultivate
57 Converse
58 Wedding vows word
59 Amazes
61 Once called
62 Merino mom

25

BY PRAVEEN GODAY

ACROSS

1 Letters often preceding a phone no.
5 Tiger with trophies
10 Environmentalist's concern
14 Elec. company
15 Shoreline feature
16 Speak (up)
17 Spy name
18 Annapolis freshman
19 Sign
20 Get steamed in the kitchen?
23 "___ we all?"
24 Lurker
25 Olympic event since 1964
28 Keystone comic
29 May honoree
32 "SOS" singers
35 Sharp gadget
37 Japanese city of 2.5 million
39 Request for attention in the kitchen?
43 Work at a wedding, perhaps
44 Age
45 Yr.-end ad word
46 Ship designation
47 Former Mideast gp.
50 Bumpkin
52 Essential
54 Salon service
58 Censure in the kitchen?
63 "Psst!"
64 Humorist Bombeck et al.
65 Precisely
66 Pitch in
67 Impertinence
68 Actress Thompson
69 Lip
70 The Magi, e.g.
71 Barely beats

DOWN

1 Ballroom dance
2 Lennon-McCartney associate
3 Curriculum ___
4 She's no Monroe
5 Cleaning cloth
6 None other than
7 Subs in tubs
8 Expose
9 Audiophile's setup
10 Frighten
11 Chevalier song
12 Economic gp. since 1960
13 Golf legend Sarazen
21 Good name for a chef?
22 Fog
26 Obstruct
27 Get credit for?
29 Palindromic address

30 Gumbo thickener
31 Gather in abundance
32 Nuts and bolts, so to speak
33 Ho-hum
34 ___ noire
36 Drano ingredient
38 "Baywatch" babe, e.g.
40 Ancient Celtic priest
41 Cry of delight
42 Verse opening
48 Swear
49 Extremely enthusiastic

51 Prehistoric prefix
52 Musical improvisations
53 Madagascar mammal
55 Ruth's mother-in-law
56 Rascal
57 Sundance's girl Place et al.
58 Angry outbursts
59 Moon of Saturn
60 Wet wigglers
61 Speed
62 "Ah, so"

26

BY BOB PEOPLES

ACROSS

1 Best bro
8 Makeshift
15 Start of a quip
16 Flier's tirade
17 Investigates carefully
18 Refreshing respites
19 Drench
20 Browned concoction
22 Inclination
23 Dash
26 Tips off
28 More of the quip
32 Aquatic players
33 Desperation tactic
38 Early first-century date
39 Affleck of "Good Will Hunting"
40 First-rate
41 Confident words
43 Among the league's best
44 End of the quip
46 Alley denizen
50 Freebies
51 Polecat ploy
52 Fling
54 Aerial enigma
57 River to Chesapeake Bay
59 Arizona product
63 Perimeter defense
64 Speaker of the quip
65 Superficial shines
66 Secures

DOWN

1 Fail to see
2 Aries or Taurus
3 "Which Way ___?": 1977 film
4 Novelist Buntline
5 Year in Alexander VI's reign
6 Put away
7 Empty-seat cause
8 Mouth
9 Oil field safety gear
10 "___ y Plata": Montana motto
11 Look into
12 One having good looks?
13 Ness was one
14 Nudniks
21 Running, swimming, etc.
23 Have on the sly
24 Matador Manolete's birthplace
25 Yelps of pain
27 Blurt out
28 Simpleton
29 1992 erupter
30 Anna of "Nana"
31 "Society's Child" singer Janis
34 Chasms
35 Sched. entry
36 Like the Gobi

37 Egg on
39 Performance
42 Screwball
43 Affiliate
45 Have a pen for a pad?
46 Lay of the land: Abbr.
47 Two-time N.L. batting champ Lefty
48 Words to live by
49 Cuts short

53 Performances
54 Beehive State college team
55 Song ending?
56 Important grain
58 Cal. pages
60 Hoosegow
61 Wriggly fish
62 Road infraction, briefly

1	2	3	4	5	6	7		8	9	10	11	12	13	14
15								16						
17								18						
19					20	21				22				
		23	24	25				26	27					
28	29	30				31								
32					33				34	35	36	37		
38				39				40						
41			42				43							
		44			45									
46	47	48	49			50								
51				52	53					54	55	56		
57			58				59	60	61	62				
63							64							
65							66							

27

BY RICHARD CHISHOLM

ACROSS
1 Refuse
6 Injure badly
10 Area
14 Mature
15 Quattro maker
16 Completed
17 Goofed
18 Rum drink
19 "The Persistence of Memory" painter
20 Visited
21 Angry city?
23 Unabashed sentimentality
25 Beverage order
26 Pesky singer?
32 Show up
35 Little bit
36 Cake ___
37 Prod
38 Air conditioner no.
39 1958 Rosalind Russell role
40 Sphere
41 "... I ___ wed"
43 Crowns
45 Province overrun with antelope?
48 Security group created under HST
49 Actress Bening

53 "Good going!," to a geologist?
58 Big part
59 Iranian bread?
60 Like the Sonora
61 Coconut Grove locale
62 Farm unit
63 Increase
64 Commencement
65 Relax, as rules
66 Hip ending
67 They're drawn in bars

DOWN
1 Take by force
2 ABC or NBC
3 Unrestrained episode
4 Like many a Selena Gomez fan
5 Complete
6 Attractive type
7 Atmosphere
8 Altar promises
9 Possibly won't
10 Collection of signs
11 Like some mirrors
12 1994 Jodie Foster film
13 Ohio native
21 Delighted
22 Star in Lyra
24 Anderson Cooper station
27 Cashed, as a forged check
28 Note to be paid
29 General Bradley

30 Capital south of Quito
31 Halves of splits?
32 Astonished
33 Having trouble deciding
34 Forbidden: Var.
38 Vaudevillian Blue
39 Actress Kahn
41 Throw
42 15th-century Hungarian cavalrymen
43 Scuba need
44 Place to stay
46 Frustrated
47 Pantry
50 Rag
51 Circus regular
52 Gets People in shape
53 Take without asking
54 French city
55 Pull down
56 Holy ___
57 Seine tributary
61 Gang

28

BY MANNY NOSOWSKY

ACROSS

1 Ball girls
5 Record number
9 Concentrate
14 "Now ___ it!"
15 Frigid finish?
16 Mess
17 Mythical sailer
18 Crawl
19 Bird with a curved neck
20 Took charge at a rapid clip?
23 Blemishes
24 They may be run at lunchtime
28 New Jersey state tree
31 Yank from the ground
32 Low voice
34 Homeowner's pride
36 Jamaica-based fictional villain
37 Make a scene?
38 Savings, and a clue to this puzzle's theme
41 Cut
42 Cut
44 Labor
45 Thrill to pieces
47 "Yay!"
49 "The Orphan Angel" author Wylie
51 Wise man
53 Prime time time
56 "Yvette's not a meat eater"?
59 Party-pooperish
62 Lighten
63 Seasoned
64 Star or ribbon
65 Scrape
66 ___-tat
67 Spells
68 Revival site
69 Fast break?

DOWN

1 Dash indicators
2 Bird that grows nuptial plumage
3 Saloon seat for Lazarus?
4 Five-cent cigars
5 Decided, period
6 Shade
7 Foot curve
8 Girlish laughter
9 Key of Mahler's Symphony No. 10
10 It has three feet
11 Diner, perhaps
12 Subj. of a sighting
13 Day light
21 Conclude with
22 Twisted with force
25 Sally Field/Bob Marley movie?
26 Prohibition beginning
27 Legree's creator
29 Plus

30 Couric of television
32 Noted musical family
33 It may come before a blessing
35 Thoroughly
39 Group character
40 Wish granter
43 Get
46 Symbol of legal scope
48 Adds to the bill
50 Create
52 A-bomb trial, for one
54 Michelangelo work
55 Reward for bravery
57 Michigan, e.g.
58 Speller's words
59 "Bad idea"
60 Use plastic
61 Send on an impulse?

29

BY CATHY MILLHAUSER

ACROSS

1 Ventura County's ___ Valley
5 Soprano Gluck
9 Love at La Scala
14 O
17 O
18 Kosher deli offering
19 Lied article
20 Caviars
21 Stir-frying need
23 Time
24 ___ Ark
27 Brooding type
30 O
36 Skye slope
37 Of hearing
38 Nautical start?
39 O
42 Yemeni port
43 Party in westerns
44 Fall guy?
47 It was dropped in the '60s
48 Heat energy meas.
49 Club dressing
52 Tuesday, in Tours
57 O
60 O
61 Book after Daniel
62 ___ Fein
63 Cold reading

DOWN

1 Like some jokes
2 Monopoly token
3 "La Bohème" seamstress
4 Doctrines
5 Abby's twin
6 Status symbol for some
7 Mid-21st-century date
8 Million-millennia period
9 Dull finish?
10 Part of MGM
11 Elvis's "The Wonder ___"
12 Less firm, maybe
13 Worser halves?
15 Christmas Eve sound
16 "The Gold Bug" author
22 Large-kitchen feature
23 Spell
24 "Eli's Coming" songwriter Laura
25 Epps of "Scream 2"
26 Laid up
27 Bugs with a gang
28 Setting of Camus's "The Plague"
29 Hydras, sea anemones, et al.
30 Compass point opposite NbE
31 Act incensed
32 Screams for teams
33 Lapidary's backlog
34 Fish-eating eagle
35 "Terrible twos" cries

40 English sum?
41 Bricklayer's laborer
44 Allergic reaction
45 Censures
46 Winged
47 Like the singin' Spoonful
48 Dinkins's predecessor
49 Mgmt. degree
50 Rounded formations
51 Himalayan legend
53 The whole enchilada
54 Abundant
55 Way out
56 Dope
58 Its cups won't hold water
59 Charged particle

30

BY D<small>IANE</small> E<small>PPERSON</small>

ACROSS

1 Shake like ___
6 Particular
10 Persian king
14 Slow movement
15 Actress Rowlands
16 Architect Saarinen
17 Triple "cross"
20 Charge
21 Latin lands
22 Cat lead-in
25 Wd. in Roget's
26 German director Wenders
27 Austin-to-Dallas dir.
28 Triple "cross"
32 Medal, e.g.
33 Dress style
34 Lake Nasser feeder
35 Market offerings
37 Sussex streetcar
41 Losing propositions?
43 Play house?
44 Triple "cross"
49 Hosp. area
50 Philosopher ___-tzu
51 Spanish article
52 Mel who hit 511 homers
53 Prepare
55 Naysayers
57 Triple "cross"

62 "A Death in the Family" author
63 Shortly
64 Shire of "The Godfather"
65 Give (out)
66 Secretary's slip
67 Hilton competitor

DOWN

1 TV alien
2 My ___, Vietnam
3 Drop the ball
4 "Ain't She Sweet?" composer
5 Concentrated
6 Williams title reptile
7 Camp sight
8 Tolkien creature
9 Popular drinks
10 Very, in Weimar
11 Words before evil
12 Richards of "Jurassic Park"
13 Fooled (around)
18 Agate variety
19 Oman neighbor
22 Kind of dive
23 "___ get it!"
24 Spoken
26 Unrestrained
29 "Judge ___": Stallone film
30 Parson's home
31 Evoking the past
35 Software dry run

36 Another, in España
38 Seat of Washoe County, Nevada
39 Work without ___
40 One of a brigantine's two
42 Lands in the ocean
43 Liqueur made with wormwood
44 Primitive dwelling
45 Period followed by melting

46 Small seed
47 Current news?
48 Oz dog
54 ___-Ball
55 Looking down, probably
56 Legal suspension
58 Coquettish
59 Schnozz ender
60 Clever one
61 Jazz cornetist Adderley

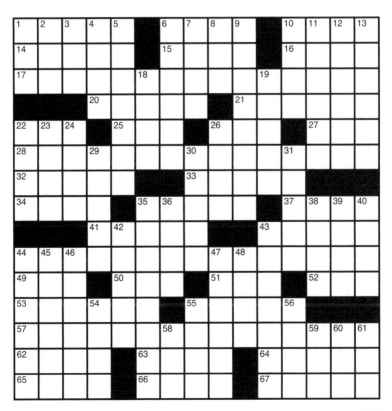

31

BY A.J. SANTORA

ACROSS

1 Blind piece
5 Boorish
10 Salute
14 Expensive
15 Laconian slave
16 Sharer's pronoun
17 Longfellow's bell town
18 Heavy and then some
19 ERA, e.g.
20 Start of a 2001 bestseller title
23 Most timid
24 Get a new crew for
27 Binary digit
28 Money-coining cost
31 Event for choosing prospects
34 Four quarters
35 Put in a hold
36 ___ tape
37 More of the title
40 Dander
41 Lago contents
43 Baddie
44 Jazz pianist Peterson
46 Shopper's destination
48 Side or straight follower
49 Play in a line
50 Nougat nuts
54 End of the title
58 Polar sheet
60 Practice piece
61 "___ la Douce"
62 Rice pad?
63 Passion
64 Continuously
65 Looking up
66 Diligent efforts
67 Break

DOWN

1 Oboe's forerunner
2 Athletic
3 Be as one
4 Imagine
5 Show a preference for
6 Disprove
7 A Baldwin
8 Fair
9 Restrain
10 Restaurant employee
11 Spontaneous
12 Savings vehicle
13 WWII vessel
21 Busybody
22 EMTs' destinations
25 Old market
26 Not that old
28 See 34-Down
29 Garden tool
30 "Exodus" hero
31 Bores
32 Palatial
33 Fans
34 With 28-Down, author of the bestseller
38 Supporting

39 Bellini opera
42 Middle Ages pseudoscience
45 More hazy
47 Work hard to get, with "out"
48 Changes
50 Building contractor's job

51 Boldness
52 Change, maybe
53 Lead off
55 Gather
56 Señora's "other"
57 A6 automaker
58 Four-term pres.
59 Head of England?

1	2	3	4		5	6	7	8	9		10	11	12	13
14					15							16			
17					18							19			
20			21							22				
23									24			25	26	
		27				28	29	30			35		
31	32	33			34					35			
36			37	38				39		40			
41		42		43				44	45				
46			47					48					
49						50				51	52	53	
	54			55	56	57						
58	59			60					61			
62				63					64			
65				66					67			

32

BY MARK DIEHL

ACROSS

1 Fat unit
5 Numskull
9 Like #1
14 Paella ingredient
15 Leif's father
16 Conductor Zubin
17 Start of a quip
20 1997 Tony winner Bebe
21 Favorite son, maybe
22 Prizm automaker
23 Baking contest entries
24 Part 2 of quip
29 Title for one tying a knot
32 Correct
33 List of stolen goods
35 Garr of "Young Frankenstein"
36 Toe woes
38 Marginal words
39 Act opener
41 Path opener?
42 "Indeed!"
43 Part 3 of quip
46 Bodybuilder's count
47 Sigma follower
48 Sick as a dog, e.g.
51 Classical language of India
56 End of the quip

58 Really bother
59 Rearview mirror ornament
60 Struggle with one's sisters?
61 Agreements
62 Disagreement
63 "Oh, dear!"

DOWN

1 Mama's mama
2 Gently sloped hill
3 Scopes Trial org.
4 Cat call
5 One of 360
6 Figure of speech?
7 Soap site
8 World Series mo.
9 Brunch fare
10 Unhip types
11 "Of ___ I Sing"
12 Amos of the '70s-'80s Kansas City Royals
13 History
18 Dark period
19 Dangerous jobs
23 Lowly laborer
24 Pretentious
25 Family female
26 Storied baddies
27 Like tissue paper
28 Disconcerted
29 Thanks, to Toulouse
30 Pine product
31 Got up
34 Clopper

36 "Leatherstocking" tales novelist
37 Load
40 Places for laces
41 It's partly melted
44 Mississippi River source
45 British medical journal, with "The"
46 Saudi coin

48 Raced
49 "Dies ___"
50 Spy name
51 Barber's cut
52 Soft drink flavoring
53 Provoke
54 "As Time Goes By" requester
55 Cookbook amts.
57 Picks from a lineup

33

BY CATHY MILLHAUSER

ACROSS

1 Barbecue utensils
6 Amahl's night visitors
10 Word in a family business name
14 Stewing
15 Kirkuk's country
16 Say it's so
17 Goats' hangouts?
19 Rock that rolls?
20 Formal impression
21 Poor, as excuses go
22 1998 Disney film
23 Marsh bird
25 Job opening
27 Distant
30 "Paper Moon" pair
34 Reddish dye
37 Nice guy's hangout?
39 Israeli submachine gun
40 China, Japan, etc.
42 Stewed
43 Beatniks' hangouts?
45 Kind of glasses
47 "Already?"
48 1953 Ladd role
50 Cancel
52 Drummers keep them
55 New Look creations
58 Iditarod terminus
61 Lacoste of tennis
63 Mouse clicker's target
64 Model's hangout?
66 ___ cava
67 Puffins' cousins
68 Ballerina Shearer
69 Bibliography abbr.
70 Choir neighbor
71 Where the Amazon begins

DOWN

1 Checks on bars
2 Village Voice awards
3 Ryan with 5,714 strikeouts
4 She played Dana on "The X-Files"
5 Crafty
6 Uris's "___ 18"
7 Kind of lily
8 Comic Kaplan and others
9 Stanford-Binet nos.
10 Tipped one's hat to
11 Lap path, often
12 Hubble subject
13 With 55-Down, bird's hangout?
18 "The People's Choice" dog
22 Hardly a good singing voice
24 Military units
26 Nottingham necessaries
28 Red sky at night, say
29 Stews
31 Fit

32 Hideout
33 Lady of Sp.
34 Bewildered utterances
35 Basso Pinza
36 Bits of booze
38 No paper cut, this
41 Posterior
44 Log
46 "Washington Merry-Go-Round" columnist
49 Help with a heist

51 Outwit
53 Lukewarm
54 Sound asleep?
55 See 13-Down
56 "Johnny Mnemonic" rapper
57 Chaplin's wife
59 Beech family members
60 Inspiring spirit
62 JFK postings
64 Ewe cry
65 Singer Sumac

34

BY KELLY CLARK

ACROSS

1 Start of a spin doctor's suggestion
8 Road clogger
15 "I need an answer now"
16 Old kitchen supplies
17 Made right
18 Disrupt
19 Carefree outing
20 Bring about
21 Church area
24 Blockhead
25 Suggestion, part 2
30 Bit of TV equipment
33 "You gonna sleep all day?" response
34 Move without effort
35 Travel to an away match?
37 Broad-minded
39 Rhapsodic
41 It means, "I believe"
42 L.A.-based oil company
44 Added
45 WWII intelligence agcy.
46 Suggestion, part 3
49 Was in session
50 Clay mixture
51 Comeback
55 Designs
60 Unexpected twists
61 Model Schiffer
63 They're happy to lose
64 Lodgings
65 As a group
66 End of the suggestion

DOWN

1 Exes appear before them
2 Rope fiber
3 Strategic WWI river
4 Ready to eat
5 Tough time
6 Wind dir.
7 Film director Browning
8 Shock
9 Table-hop, say
10 Big name in breweries
11 Big Band music
12 Ovation
13 Galvanize
14 Equal
20 Ophidian fish
22 Kind of bargain
23 Sub station?
25 Roger's follower
26 Islamic rulers
27 Bouillon shapes
28 Acted like
29 Closing material
30 Cold-weather drink
31 Separated
32 Fracas
36 Delineate
38 Strings of prayer beads
40 Luke's teacher
43 It may be leading

47 Says
48 Chevy model
49 Client of this puzzle's spin doctor?
51 Tease
52 Actress Gray
53 Pound work

54 Latin being
56 Doozy
57 Summer drinks
58 TV's "Nick at ___"
59 Fresh talk
61 Toronto TV channel
62 Dogpatch adjective

35

BY DAVID J. KAHN

ACROSS

1 Busy one
5 Stop on the road
8 Boas and such
14 "It's ___ can ask"
15 Philip VI, e.g.
16 Deck piece
17 Jessica Lange's movie debut
19 Cossack chief
20 Egg, for openers
21 Scale unit
22 Gwyneth Paltrow's movie debut
23 Coffee break hr.
25 Chopin works
28 Over
29 Gillette brand
30 Frat letter
33 Total: Abbr.
36 Truman initiative
38 Lee Remick's movie debut
42 Missing person
43 Who blows thar?
44 Swinging joint?
45 Angel or Mariner, say
46 50-and-over org.
50 Caterer's supply
52 More remarkable
53 Meryl Streep's movie debut
56 Part of Caesar's boast
58 Summer cooler
59 How some tales are told
61 Angela Lansbury's movie debut
63 The first one was shown in 1927
64 Med. exam stat
65 Losing program
66 Buffy is one
67 Sri Lanka export
68 Trinitron maker, once

DOWN

1 North ___
2 Michigan college or its city
3 Unpredictable current
4 Manipulate
5 Club at a club
6 Time being
7 Mae West's movie debut
8 Acad.
9 Montgomery Clift's movie debut
10 Swear words
11 Fancy wheels
12 Birthright seller
13 E-mailed
18 Actress Basinger
24 Quickly
26 Four Corners state
27 Hardens, perhaps
30 Popular '20s auto
31 Hem partner

32 Dated
34 Al Pacino's movie debut
35 Mr. or Mrs.
37 Trepidation
38 Circus cry
39 Justice gp.
40 Cleo's undoing
41 ___-do-well
47 Slowly
48 "Little" fictional critter
49 Quite
50 Lustrous
51 Siouan language
52 Hooter
53 Writes
54 Orenburg's river
55 Singing syllables
57 Charles barker
60 Law closing?
62 Recognizes

36

BY MANNY NOSOWSKY

ACROSS

1 Laughingstock
5 Score number
9 Kind of engr.
13 Dizzying genre
15 The greater number
16 Nautical direction
17 Guest of poetry
18 Lhasa ___
19 Brick oven
20 Poster woman of WWII
23 "As I was saying ..."
24 Visited
25 Big wheel at sea
27 Race distance
29 "Half ___ is better ..."
31 Turn's partner
32 Watched the kids
35 Hank Ketcham creation
39 Classic sports car, informally
40 Zap
41 Amiens is its capital
42 Tropical trees
45 "Yes!"
46 Type of hiring discrimination
49 City on the Hudson
51 Thief of verse
55 Exec
56 Surrealist influenced by Freud
57 Greeted the day
58 Della's creator
59 Informed of
60 Desert rises
61 City first mentioned in Ezekiel
62 Cut a bit
63 Sunbeams

DOWN

1 Transvaal settler
2 High style
3 Decides to go (with)
4 Casey Jones, e.g.
5 Fred Astaire, by birth
6 Olive fancier
7 Soyuz launcher
8 Zeno's philosophy
9 Schoolyard challenge
10 Top-drawer
11 Paparazzi's quarry
12 Ford or Hudson
14 Hardly a big heart?
21 Bit or part lead-in
22 Ravel dancelike works
25 Holy pilgrimage
26 Zeno's home
28 '50s-'70s pitcher Drabowsky
30 Wind up
32 2000 N.L. home run champ
33 Summit
34 High schooler, e.g.
36 Recapitulated
37 Fight ender

38 Comment made while hanging up, maybe

42 Warmer on a string

43 Skiing category

44 Direction opposite NbW

46 Uncertain

47 Small-necked bottle

48 "South Pacific" hero

50 Saroyan title character

52 Bear name

53 Fine

54 Loch with a legend

37

BY LYNN LEMPEL

ACROSS

1 Iditarod racers
6 Increases the speed of, with "up"
10 Glowing circle
14 Sound
15 Foot feature
16 Verve
17 College e-mail #1: yawn!
20 Collection pit
21 Adds to
22 Some migrations
23 "___ House": Graham Nash song
25 Account
27 College e-mail #2: yuck!
35 "I am Fortune's fool" speaker
36 Tiger's domain
37 Vane dir.
38 Actress Gardner
39 Smart player
40 Retardation
41 "Little Women" woman
42 Staging ground
43 Hot Swedish wine beverage
45 College e-mail #3: help!
48 Harvard req. for some
49 Catchall abbr.
50 Vermont state tree
53 Sprite
55 Feared snakes
59 College e-mail #4: surprise!
63 Meter reading
64 Ornamental vases
65 Cry of success
66 Stew
67 "Uh-huh"
68 Flub

DOWN

1 Follicles, e.g.
2 Corker
3 Mild cheese
4 Get rid (of)
5 It may be tapped out
6 Grating sound
7 Historians' subjects
8 Taper?
9 "Ain't ___ Sweet"
10 Moses, for one
11 Burn remedy
12 Symbol of happiness
13 People
18 Multinational money
19 One of the Titans
24 Roswell sighting
25 Scarecrow associate
26 Shows curiosity
27 Lady's partner
28 Shack
29 Representation
30 Least fresh
31 "Cheers" waitress

32 Cop's quarry
33 Dictionary topic
34 Like many a model
39 It may be gray
42 Plus
43 Clock-setting std.
44 Private eye, at times
46 Ready
47 Skillful
50 Annoy

51 Not fully closed
52 Virtuous
53 Sicilian landmark
54 Bind with rope
56 Commotion
57 Kind of shirt
58 Rise rapidly
60 Chap
61 It's found in veins
62 Caesar's welcome

1	2	3	4	5		6	7	8	9		10	11	12	13
14						15					16			
17				18					19					
20				21				22						
			23	24			25	26						
27	28	29			30	31					32	33	34	
35					36					37				
38				39						40				
41			42					43	44					
45			46				47							
			48					49						
50	51	52				53	54			55	56	57	58	
59				60	61			62						
63				64				65						
66				67				68						

38

BY PAULA GAMACHE

ACROSS
1 Like a gossip's tongue
5 Learning method
9 Verbal barbs
14 Not at all well done
15 Some court opponents
16 "Lonely Nights" singer Bryan
17 ___ mater
18 WWII singer ___ Lynn
19 Jungle knives
20 Fictional Irish caveman?
23 It's charged
24 Choler
25 Volcanic rock
28 Each
30 Oft-needed-info list
32 Supportive sound
33 Affable
35 Nastiness
37 Ho-hum after-school activity?
40 Sea
41 Silver ___
42 "___ Woman": Reddy hit
43 Teensy
44 Dealt
48 Frequent Johnny Carson guest
51 Sallie ___
52 Travelers' org.

53 Zero balances?
57 Start of a dedicatory title
59 Winter Olympics event
60 Silence
61 Cohort of Doc
62 Ruins site near the Gulf of Salerno
63 Tony relative
64 Lotte of "From Russia with Love"
65 Fall place
66 Female lobsters

DOWN
1 Asian peninsula
2 Defeat utterly
3 Versace rival
4 Reverse, for one
5 Clerical title
6 Daisy variety
7 Yukon, e.g.: Abbr.
8 Grandson of Abraham
9 "Return of the Jedi" villain
10 Favorites
11 ___ Islands: Majorca's chain
12 Comedian Philips
13 Gp. that had a lottery
21 ___ Creed
22 Short grill?
26 Held up, in a way
27 Article in Time
29 Alaska's first governor
30 Travesty

31 Wing-shaped
34 ___ dixit
35 Multi-channel system
36 ___ colada
37 Tops
38 Food named for a national capital
39 Whale or dolphin
40 Profession, casually
43 Colorless
45 Black Sea feeder

46 Has leftovers, say
47 Sprints
49 Polish money
50 Seasonal figure
51 Fibber of radio
54 "Twittering Machine" artist
55 New Year's word
56 "Oops"
57 Symbol of wisdom
58 Do root work, perhaps

39

BY ELIZABETH C. GORSKI

ACROSS
1 Laughing ___
4 Irk
9 Sensitivity
13 "Phooey!"
15 Chicle source
16 Confess
17 Horne solo
18 Cool time in Cádiz
19 "Catch a Falling Star" singer
20 Start of a quip
22 Till fillers
23 Deduce
24 Amy, to Meg or Jo
26 Home land?
27 Mountain road feature
28 Radio type
32 Beach convenience
34 "Compromising Positions" author
36 Rock bottom
37 Celebrity to whom the quip is attributed
40 Of a forearm bone
41 Soup bean
42 Hurt badly
44 North Carolina motto beginning
45 AWOL pursuers
48 English VIPs
49 Add
51 Leave
53 Mid-month time
55 End of the quip
59 Justice Bader Ginsburg
60 Talk tiringly
61 Former talk show name
62 Prefix with derm
63 Dark
64 Major finale?
65 Depict unfairly
66 Lacking luster
67 "Mayday!"

DOWN
1 George's love
2 ___ rod
3 Lucky ones?
4 Merriment
5 Indian dignitary
6 Roscoe of old Westerns
7 Shore fliers
8 Like Fantasy Island
9 Tijuana treat
10 She makes a lot of calls
11 "It's open!"
12 Like a major general
14 Wall unit, perhaps
21 Some corrections
25 Pacific Highway city
29 West of Hollywood
30 Drop
31 Fictional detective Travis ___
33 Break down, in a way
34 Islamic priest

35 '60s–'70s sitcom trio
37 Dramatic court maneuver
38 Sweet cordial
39 OCS grads
40 Home rulers?
43 Pinhead
45 William Byrd works

46 Spanish port
47 Score lines
50 Loy of "Broadway Bill"
52 "All ___": 1931 tune
54 Point out
56 Inventor Samuel
57 Module
58 Sneaky guy?

40

BY LEONARD WILLIAMS

ACROSS

1 Born in
5 "Roots" and others
10 Beliefs
14 Dynamic prelude
15 Like some entertainment
16 Immerse
17 Ness underlings
18 Mondavi competitor
19 Charlie Brown associate
20 Ineffective bedding?
23 Drifting, maybe
24 Social
25 Welcomer
28 Souvenir shop item
29 Bio relative
33 All too willing
35 Coming from at least two sources
37 "Family Ties" role
38 Bedroom art lesson?
43 Mystique
44 Soup vegetables
45 With intensity
48 Astonish
49 Corn Belt st.
52 Football's Parseghian
53 Cary's "North By Northwest" costar
55 With respect to
57 Bedtime reading?

62 Tell companion
64 Collection
65 Not behind
66 Auxiliary
67 Shades
68 Coalition
69 Garden problem
70 Decorative vessels
71 Holiday song word

DOWN

1 Plutocrat supporter
2 Scene changer of a sort
3 Threat ender
4 Parisian daily, with "Le"
5 Palm starch
6 Eliot's "___ Bede"
7 Chasm
8 Dole out
9 Put away
10 Sailor's observation
11 Coffee spoiler
12 Buddy
13 Place to see Superman
21 Desert vista
22 Eastern way
26 Sheltered, in a way
27 Course requirement
30 Layer
31 Cartesian conjunction
32 Method
34 Axes
35 Switch
36 Final story?
38 Arp's art

39 Contrite one
40 727 in Florida, e.g.
41 Comical Costello
42 Actress Paquin and others
46 Bk. after Exodus
47 Actress Mimieux
49 Words of hindsight
50 Carney role

51 Refrigerant trademark
54 Road sign symbol
56 Attempts
58 Was obligated
59 Unassisted
60 At any time
61 Mrs. Dick Tracy
62 Dated
63 Go in haste

41

BY DAVID J. KAHN

ACROSS

1 Start of a query
9 Query, part 2
15 More vigorous
16 Weakness
17 Stray, maybe
18 In a functional way
19 Kid
20 Running mate of 29-Down
22 Prohibitionists
23 Try
25 Journal ending
26 Kind of juice?
27 Needing to be closed, perhaps
30 Query, part 3
34 Neptune, for one
37 Sponsorship: Var.
38 The Smothers Brothers, e.g.
39 Outback critter
40 Query, part 4
42 Break off
43 "Collages" novelist
44 Unaffectedness
45 Orderly, persuasive, sociable types, presumably
47 Query, part 5
49 Art follower?
50 "Deck the Halls" contraction
51 It's unhittable
53 Banned pollutants
57 Vingt-___: blackjack
59 Convene again
62 Sound of delight
63 Shunned one
66 Secondary pursuit
68 Conceive
69 Priced individually
70 Query, part 6
71 End of the query

DOWN

1 "___ up?"
2 Ancient serf
3 Black Sea port
4 Pique
5 Eye ailment
6 Peculiarities
7 Hood's rod
8 Art pieces by Romain de Tirtoff
9 Sigma follower
10 Those elected
11 Grassy area
12 Do needlework
13 Like cold cream
14 Wray and Weldon
21 Marsh plant
24 Catch
26 Connecticut tourist town
28 Painter Albers et al.

29 Ike adversary
31 Pew access
32 Albacore, for one
33 Coal carriers
34 FedExed
35 Kuwaiti dignitary
36 In the buff
37 Sheepish one?
41 Actor's honor
46 Conk
48 Gable adornment
49 1957 RKO purchaser

52 Composer Franck
54 View from Giza
55 Language group that includes Swahili
56 Out-and-out
57 Like some proportions
58 "I did it!"
60 Lupino and Tarbell
61 Georgia ____
64 Took in
65 "____ be a fool not to!"
67 ____-di-dah

42

BY SARAH KELLER

ACROSS

1 H.S. exam for top students
7 "Tell ___ the Marines"
11 Treatment for the blues, briefly
14 Nap
15 Fen-___: controversial diet drug combo
16 Hope-Crosby destination
17 Repressed
18 Whenever
20 Capitalist principle
22 Lode find
23 ___ Miguel, largest of the Azores
24 Barcelona bread
26 Break
28 Map abbr.
30 Drillers' org.
31 Mass
34 Went on and on
37 Agree
39 Lake Kyoga locale
41 Wine type
42 Dine
43 "___ was saying ..."
44 Actress Thompson
48 Authorize
52 Depression era prog.
55 Hardy
56 Brunch serving
59 Buccaneers' milieu
60 Plagiarist
61 Long time, to Longfellow
62 ___ monster
63 One of a '50s brothers team
64 Measurement found in 20-, 37-, and 56-Across
65 Preliminary contest
66 Wasteland

DOWN

1 Request
2 Capital on the Missouri
3 Simple dwellings
4 Villa d'___
5 Farm enclosures
6 Urich's "Vega$" role
7 ___ dixit
8 Legendary Native American athlete Jim
9 Home of the Sun Devils
10 Humdingers
11 Like Greater New York
12 Summer cooler
13 Miler Sebastian
19 Even
21 Sycophant
25 Blue
27 Afterward
29 Avoids an accident, maybe

32 Large ref. work
33 "Citizen X" actor
34 Hawaiian staple
35 Toon dog
36 Affirmatives
37 Corundum gem
38 Whatsis
39 In ___: occupied
40 Kookaburra's roost, in a kid's song
43 Biological ring
45 Fiery

46 One with a losing attitude?
47 Confirm, with "to"
49 Former western fort
50 Examine
51 Like many a Halloween costume
53 Caught, in a way
54 LSD, for one
57 Little pest
58 Baseball stats
59 "Really!"

43

BY ROBERT H. WOLFE

ACROSS

1 Workout targets
5 More than talk
9 Zealous
14 Major test
15 University of Nevada site
16 "___ traveller ...": Shelley
17 Katz of "Hocus Pocus"
18 State openly
19 Famous
20 Cover a water source, in Greece?
22 Growls
23 Still wrapped
24 Close
25 Needle providers
26 Give solace
29 Lake sight
33 Exertion
34 Fellow
37 Ideal
39 Answer book
40 Song and dance
42 Terrible
44 Grouping
46 Ecological community
50 Musical with the song "Good Morning Starshine"
51 Basic particle

54 Easy gaits
56 Gave cards, in Greece?
57 Affects adversely
58 Singer Adams
59 Pale brown
60 Meet with again
61 Church area
62 Gin flavoring
63 Some hackers
64 Husky trailer
65 Summer garments

DOWN

1 Research
2 Minimalist Italian designer
3 Game fish
4 Prince's find, in a fairy tale
5 Strength
6 Mississippi feature
7 "___ Fashioned Love Song": 1971 hit
8 Rose ___
9 Greet, as the new year
10 In the middle of
11 Prepare to fish, in Greece?
12 Roman way
13 Pops
21 Noted storyteller
24 "___ This Earth": sci-fi film
26 "Con Air" star

27 Rest
28 English city near Cambridge
30 Ibis, for one
31 Telly watcher
32 It may be in a lock
34 Ring tactic
35 1967 NHL Rookie of the Year
36 Pigged out, in Greece?
38 Ancient northern African region
41 Spread out

43 Most flexible
45 Chocolate treats
47 Prophet
48 "Camel Caravan" bandleader Vaughan ___
49 Assumes, as a role
51 Piano part
52 Yellowish green
53 Silver, e.g.
54 By way of, for short
55 Feels sorrow about
56 They have mothers

44

BY MANNY NOSOWSKY

ACROSS

1 See 37-Across
11 Cut
15 Cranky
16 Larger-than-life
17 Be honored posthumously
18 Indian music
19 Fort near Louisville
20 Men
21 "Play it, Sam" speaker
22 "I agree"
23 Lake ___ Vista: gateway to Disney World
25 Had a little lamb
26 Would like
27 Ford fuel
29 Lock (up)
32 Crawling
35 Lickable treat
37 Founder of group for which 62-Across is the 1-Across
39 Introduced gradually
40 Rubbed off
41 Drench
42 "Michael Collins" actor
43 Taps
44 "Mystery!" broadcaster
46 Secluded homes
48 Second Amendment supporters: Abbr.

51 Vicinity
53 Mikita of the NHL
54 "My Country" author
55 Rather's CBS News predecessor
56 Cool
59 Put ___ in one's ear
60 Being attacked
61 Play up to the max
62 See 37-Across

DOWN

1 Smooth
2 "Crazy" singer
3 Bread spreads
4 Early computer operating system
5 Summer shade
6 High spots: Abbr.
7 Get-go
8 Bride follower
9 Rectangle or square
10 Lofty lines
11 With 45-Down, award in 37-Across's group
12 Sparkles with color
13 Halloween props
14 Sports org. since 1906
23 Owners of clippers
24 Like a dorm bed, probably
25 Arranges
26 Bills galore
28 Show
30 Paris pronoun
31 Make joints, in a way

32 Brenner Pass locale
33 London district
34 Concluded
35 Write thing
36 "___ Made to Love Her": Wonder hit
38 Landline feature
43 Lobster claw
45 See 11-Down
47 Grand Union competitor

48 Cager, on the sports page
49 Oven
50 Prepared for a deal
51 Asian nursemaid
52 Lipstick shade
53 Put down
54 Oscar-winner Kazan
57 Louis I's realm: Abbr.
58 Nile biter

45

BY LYNN LEMPEL

ACROSS

1 Wake-up call
6 Dull
10 Skater Lipinski
14 Santa ___
15 Function
16 Subject of adoration
17 Start of a paraphrased quip by Natalie Wood
20 Span. title
21 It may precede a shot
22 Subject
23 "___ Brockovich"
24 "Evita" role
25 Quip, part 2
30 Apiece, in game scores
33 Scrounges
34 Like some parts of compounds
36 Kind of pool
37 Did a restaurant job
39 Side
40 Mushroom, e.g.
42 1836 siege site
43 Lansing-to-Detroit dir.
44 Quip, part 3
47 Denials
48 Chats
49 Erasmus's burial site
52 Fury
54 Visitors' center handout
57 End of the quip

60 Carry
61 Noodle
62 Cold-weather-wear unit
63 Hindu's "sir"
64 Crooked
65 Business

DOWN

1 Tsp. and tbsp.
2 "If I Were the King of the Forest" singer
3 Geometry calculation
4 River in Toledo
5 Chanted words
6 Football coach with 323 lifetime wins
7 Mobs
8 Dismounted
9 Take up, maybe
10 Church support
11 Yearning
12 Meander
13 Fixed stake
18 Pork cut
19 ___ acetate
23 Glowing bit
24 Bumbler
25 Banded marble
26 Songbirds
27 Light weight
28 Escalated
29 Resort to
30 At right angles to the keel
31 Andes traveler
32 Sidecar flavoring

35 Reference section offering
37 Dissatisfied remarks
38 NAFTA signer
41 School abroad
42 Road crew's supply
45 Like old newsreels
46 Noshes
47 Indian independence leader

49 Lettuce variety
50 Cruising
51 Tar
52 "Thank goodness!"
53 Bring up
54 Early Yucatán settler
55 Sleeping, most likely
56 Rite pile
58 Bulls' org.
59 Exclude

46

BY WILL KNORR

ACROSS
1 Burger embellishment
6 Suspect's story
11 Woman
14 Choose the window instead of the aisle?
15 Emergency sign
16 And not
17 Start of a question
20 Amphilochus, for one
21 Desires
22 They might be high
23 It covers some ground
25 Like many reprimands
26 Question, part 2
31 No place for a bum steer
32 Charleson of "Chariots of Fire"
33 Pool accessory
37 ___ order
38 Ready
42 Outlaw
43 Squeezes (out)
45 Matterhorn, e.g.
46 Past pudgy
48 Question, part 3
52 Promise
55 Rebuke from Caesar
56 Golf club part
57 Sport with horses
59 Others
63 End of the question

66 Wrath
67 1984 Texaco acquisition
68 Showed "Cheers," say
69 "___ now or never"
70 Those unconcerned with the bottom line?
71 Shangri-las

DOWN
1 Nap sacks
2 Tissue ingredient
3 Manage
4 Manage
5 New beginning?
6 Nodding
7 Property claim
8 Pupil's place
9 Big ___
10 Narrow margin
11 Take potshots
12 One with an ax to grind
13 Wipe out
18 Site of a phoenix's demise
19 Be overattentive, as a waiter
24 A little lamb?
25 Having all of one's marbles
26 Compulsion
27 Drench
28 Postcards source?
29 River horse
30 Snoop Dogg's genre
34 Case the joint, e.g.

35 Green
36 The "genu" in "genuflect"
39 Give a 9.5, say
40 Sprite
41 Blockhead
44 Good thing to be up to
47 Indistinct
49 Spanish philosopher José ___ y Gasset
50 Passes on
51 Speck

52 Computer storage acronym
53 Testy
54 Targets for crackers
57 "Seven Years in Tibet" actor
58 Informed of
60 Sinn Fein's land
61 Doctor's order
62 Browns
64 That's a moray
65 Poetic preposition

1	2	3	4	5		6	7	8	9	10		11	12	13
14						15						16		
17				18						19				
20				21					22					
		23	24				25							
26	27	28				29	30							
31						32				33	34	35	36	
37			38	39	40				41		42			
43			44		45					46	47			
		48	49				50	51						
52	53	54					55							
56						57	58				59	60	61	62
63				64					65					
66				67					68					
69				70					71					

47

BY PAULA GAMACHE

ACROSS

1 Drudge
5 Soybean paste
9 Says, "I'll be there," perhaps
14 Prefix with dollar
15 Over
16 Medium board
17 2000 Oscar-winning role for Julia
18 Examine hastily
19 Smallest
20 Guinevere's gam?
23 Downhill runner
24 Escape
25 Fish stick?
26 Jazz gp.
29 Irate biological class?
33 Conscious
34 French naval missile
35 Oveta Culp Hobby's WWII underlings
38 Plus
40 Goose egg
41 Slip by
44 Confiscate
47 No-nonsense contrapuntal melodies?
51 Part of PST: Abbr.
52 ___ pro nobis
53 Summit
54 New NYSE issue

56 "It'll never stop," and this puzzle's title
59 Ring used in a horseshoelike game
62 Completely cooked
63 Worry
64 "Tyger! Tyger! burning bright" poet
65 Riviera seasons
66 Cause for an alarm
67 Less dangerous
68 Katharine of "The Graduate"
69 North Sea feeder

DOWN

1 Strips away
2 Literally, "I have found it!"
3 Inception
4 Words to Nanette?
5 Revlon offering
6 Without an audience, to a judge
7 Mine line
8 Proprietors
9 Office filing aid
10 Mincemeat fat
11 Itinerary word
12 Jammies
13 Rested, maybe
21 Piloted
22 More than a trot
26 Riviera resort
27 Root ___
28 Concerning

30 Quebec town on its own peninsula
31 Obtuse
32 Deceive
35 Ties the knot
36 Got off
37 Check the ID of, as in a bar
39 Preordains
42 Two-wheeler
43 Sartre's being
45 Hardly a good reception

46 Nukes
48 It's up when you're upset
49 Baghdad's river
50 Area of influence
55 Playful swimmer
56 Adidas rival
57 Impose upon
58 Up in the air
59 NFL leaders
60 Form finish
61 Klutz

48

BY ANNE GARELLICK

ACROSS

1 Allen successor
5 Just above average
10 Pest
14 Alençon is its capital
15 Get up
16 Prefix with biology
17 Early traveler to America
18 Pool stroke
19 Make baba, e.g.
20 Definition of grandchildren, part 1
23 "Born in the ___"
24 Two or more eras
25 Cedar repels them
28 Samples
30 A little night music?
33 "So there!"
34 Stand for knickknacks
37 It's creepy
38 Definition, part 2
41 Swindles
42 Brunch orders
43 Mature
44 "The ___ Must Be Crazy": 1980s film
45 Snug retreats
49 Cook with books
51 Gossip
53 Driver's aid
54 End of definition

59 School on the Thames
61 Patrick of the NBA
62 Predatory dolphin
63 One of a Latin trio
64 Starr and Simpson
65 Appear to be
66 Suit
67 "Save me ___"
68 Dig it

DOWN

1 Settle a debt
2 Melodic
3 Marigold, e.g.
4 Back
5 Relief-design jewelry
6 Shrimp relative
7 "Stay" singer Loeb
8 Red letters?
9 Germ
10 Forbidden
11 Ebb, as patience
12 Irritate
13 Low digit
21 Gets a little refreshment
22 Radio choices
26 Suspend
27 Ewe, for one
29 "Sure, why not?"
30 Farm haulers
31 Italian flower
32 Throws
35 Sphere head?
36 Place for plotting
37 Carpentry tool
38 Canceled, at NASA

39 Single file
40 Sri ___
41 Part of a train
44 Wildebeest
46 Sound investment?
47 Old Toyota
48 Bagel flavoring
50 Architectural order
51 Busybody

52 Kierkegaard subject
55 First name in country
56 "___ the night before ..."
57 Green land
58 "Wow"
59 Woman's name meaning "life"
60 John Ritter's dad

49

BY SARAH KELLER

ACROSS

1 Ganders, e.g.
6 Proceed effortlessly
11 Diamond arbiter
14 Barcelona buddy
15 Burning
16 Scand. land
17 Start of a quip
19 Half an injury?
20 N.H. hours
21 American Legion member
22 Hammer parts
24 Has on
26 Soft drink choice
27 Quip, part 2
32 Ledger entry
33 Inlet
34 Principal
35 FedEx rival
36 Supreme Court Justice, 1975-2010
40 Spoiled
41 Cigar end
43 Actress Meyers
44 Matches a bet
46 Quip, part 3
50 Dos follower
51 Exhilarate
52 Swampy areas
54 Acct. addition
55 Back (out)

58 Clay, today
59 End of the quip
64 Recurring blink, maybe
65 Mecca native
66 Croupiers' needs
67 Holds
68 ___ clef
69 Used bread?

DOWN

1 Fixed, as a meal
2 "1000 Oceans" singer Tori
3 Raise
4 Self-importance
5 Acetone and alcohol
6 Old convertible name
7 Not up to snuff
8 Life support
9 Sign of a seating shortage
10 Maestro's concerns
11 Excruciating
12 Full ___
13 NFLers, e.g.
18 New Zealand parrots
23 Type of sch.
24 It began 7/28/1914
25 Outlive
26 Sidney Toler role
27 Ocean figure
28 Delivery field
29 Even
30 Serum holders

31 Wraps up
32 Tune for two
37 Filing aids
38 Before, to bards
39 Disperses
42 Dublin's land
45 Scotch bottle datum
47 Oppose
48 Cure-all
49 Hindu princess

52 It has its pluses and minuses
53 Pelvic bones
55 Squash relative, briefly
56 Begin
57 Verbal nudge
60 Burns not?
61 Bradstreet partner
62 Swear words?
63 Noodle topper

50

BY MITCH KOMRO

ACROSS

1 Narrow the gap
5 Family members
9 Teacher's assignment
14 Another, in Oviedo
15 Parmenides's home
16 Actor Ian et al.
17 Red-bearded god
18 Distinctive flair
19 Holiday visitor, perhaps
20 Zoologist's start-up?
23 Latin lover's verb
24 Angus's refusal
25 Bridge positions
27 Impressions
29 Laugh syllable
31 Mordant Mort
32 Comme ci, comme ça
36 Familia member
37 Prophet's start-up?
40 Bygone auto feature
41 Loved
42 "What Women Want" actor
44 Subordinates of capts.
45 Lands in water
49 Tube
51 RN's concerns
53 Antlered beast
54 Santa's start-up?
58 Bowling sites
59 Smell ___
60 Homeric
61 Oklahoma tribe
62 Stable parent
63 Yakutsk's river
64 Eye sores
65 Fired
66 Gift tag word

DOWN

1 Burned
2 In
3 Patch type
4 Stoolie, in Sussex
5 "Later, dude!"
6 "Well, ___!"
7 Regular date
8 ___-culotte: revolutionary
9 Pants fabric
10 Mavericks
11 Like top high school athletes
12 Huge success
13 Waco-to-Austin dir.
21 Endow with spiritual awareness
22 Forced entry
26 ___-pitch
28 Big bang cause
29 MDs' milieus
30 [Sigh!]
33 Irish seaport of song
34 Cal. page
35 Cliché
37 March by singly

38 No longer at rest
39 Mil. cooking help
40 Thick
43 Right, as a wrong
46 Gymnast, at times
47 Current news?
48 Bird's-eye view offerer

50 Tough curves
51 Words of support
52 Opted
55 Columbia launcher
56 Cereal "for kids"
57 Ill-gotten gains
58 ___ Alamos

51

BY DON WEST

ACROSS

1 Generous sort
6 Mineral springs
10 Greater
14 Run for your wife?
15 Lyre's cousin
16 In a bit
17 Vanquishes
18 Asian sea
19 "Cool"
20 Succeed
23 Syrupy
25 Wall Street regular
26 Sir Galahad's mother
27 Intention
29 Show stoppers?
30 Scarlett's spread
31 Defensive efforts
33 Succeed
37 Marked by formality
38 Soft drink choice
41 Sternward
44 Does some yard work
45 Loose overcoat
47 Brooches
49 Scoldings
50 Succeed
53 R&B singer James
54 Type
55 Gem State capital
58 Frank server
59 In addition
60 Cruise ship
61 Macmillan's predecessor
62 Socials
63 Bed neatener

DOWN

1 Ball girl
2 ___ Miss
3 Setting in the musical "Two By Two"
4 They make a lot of contacts
5 Pulitzer-winning journalist James
6 Persian kings
7 Peel
8 Middle East native
9 Quarterback's target
10 Ray in the sea
11 Iroquois Confederacy tribe
12 Wandered
13 Logs
21 Calendar col.
22 Incline
23 Old-timer
24 Waterfront union: Abbr.
27 List parts
28 Butler's last word
31 Bias
32 Equanimity
34 Vitality
35 Like some villainous eyes

36 Misleading
39 Actor Holbrook
40 Gp. that issued green cards
41 Assent (to)
42 Grooved, as a column
43 Squeal
45 Squeal

46 Suitable for farming
48 Spot to get off
49 Former Tennessee senator Kefauver
51 Skin blemish
52 ___ Minor
56 Spot
57 Drop the ball

52

BY SHERRY O. BLACKARD

ACROSS

1 Lemons
5 They're caught at the beach
9 Trapshooting
14 Stat opener
15 Stick used in cooking
16 What stripes do with checks
17 "The Green Mile," literarily
19 Right-hand page
20 Place for a needle
21 "The Asphalt Jungle," literarily
23 Convened
24 Bush press secretary Fleischer
26 Choose
27 "Chitty Chitty Bang Bang," literarily
33 Novelist Clavell
36 Showy flower
37 Boiling
38 Humbled
39 Byes
40 Vaudeville brothers
41 Resolve
42 Works one's way up
43 Blender setting
44 "Twice-Told Tales," literarily

47 Facetiously innocent response
48 Revue since '75
49 Alphabet trio
52 "True Lies," literarily
57 Gompers or Goldwyn
59 Prepare to drive
60 "20,000 Leagues Under the Sea," literarily
62 Ridiculous
63 Hot bed
64 Leave ___
65 Felt compassion
66 Inventor Elisha
67 Faction

DOWN

1 Riffraff
2 "Star Trek" communications officer
3 Stop on a line
4 Area north of Piccadilly Circus
5 The Joker portrayer
6 1996 Olympic cauldron lighter
7 Tom Sawyer agreement
8 One or more
9 Feisty
10 One to watch in a pinch?
11 A pop
12 This, in Tijuana
13 God with a hammer
18 Dwight of the '70s-'80s-'90s Red Sox
22 Hanna-Barbera creations

25 Damage
27 Ref. conceived in 1857
28 State Farm competitor
29 Party lines?
30 Dubai leader
31 "Must've been something ___"
32 Cutting tool
33 Mug filler
34 MP's quarry
35 Feeble cry
39 "... over ___ flock by night": Luke
40 Take off
42 Bent

43 Opposite in character
45 Protected
46 Some city maps
49 Repeat verbatim
50 Keepsake
51 Delayed deciding (on)
52 Ending for psych
53 Lawless character?
54 Word with end or round
55 "Say it isn't so!"
56 Nikita's no
58 Some CEOs
61 "___ Love You": Beatles hit

53

BY LILA CHERRY

ACROSS
1 Jam
6 Casino pursuit
11 Frat letter
14 Opening bit
15 1944 Preminger classic
16 Not at all nerdy
17 Primate leader?
19 Police blotter entry
20 Flipper
21 Reach the beach
22 Urge forward
24 Light-haired trash dealers?
27 Monastic jurisdiction
30 Multitudes
33 Coffee order
34 Unstable leptons
36 Slight decrease
37 Use a machete
38 Capital east of Seoul
39 Best Picture winner of 1958
40 Sitcom planet
41 Founded
42 Case, perhaps
43 News agency since 1851
45 Dies (out)
46 Fender bender?
49 Really keyed up
51 Cryptic character
52 NRC forerunner

55 Distress
56 This puzzle's title
60 FDR program
61 Expanding agent
62 1998 A.L. Manager of the Year
63 Understanding
64 Like many chips
65 Less forward

DOWN
1 Spat
2 Crucifix inscription
3 Thames college
4 Still-life subject
5 Church supper, maybe
6 Low, dull sound
7 Ray Charles's genre
8 Black-and-white diver
9 Start for serve or shrink
10 Maxims
11 Speak with great enthusiasm
12 Backpack, e.g.
13 Fall birthstone
18 Scores
23 Early 16th-century date
24 London or Lord
25 Actor Nolan
26 Napa prefix
27 Can't stand
28 Raucous sound
29 It's just in case
31 River through Mali
32 Short drives
34 Like some wet ground

35 Island entertainment
38 Sharp
39 Fourth-century invader
41 Acts disloyally
42 They may be just
44 Souvenir shop item
45 Throb
47 Highest point
48 Like many dirt roads
49 Peddle
50 "Oh, no!"
52 Wrong
53 Burgundy being
54 "Dark Lady" singer
57 Large amount
58 Baseball's Bando
59 "Gosh!"

54

BY BRUCE VENZKE

ACROSS

1 Expel with force
5 Settle, as a bill
9 Pool stroke
14 French artist Bonheur
15 Accomplished
16 Haughty
17 A tale of morning woes: first the ___
20 "Apparently"
21 Health resort
22 JFK predictions
23 Writer Oz
25 Cube makeup
27 Then the ___
35 Tokyo's former name
36 Lead
37 Relish
38 Unreliable witness
40 Military metaphor
43 Make over
44 Ghostly
46 Opinion
48 Dreamer's acronym
49 And the ___
53 Name in an historic '70s case
54 Box or bucket follower
55 Flock noises
59 Flee
61 Attack from above
65 And when I finally got there, the ___!
68 Bette's "All About Eve" role
69 Fever and shivering
70 More than slow, in retail
71 Kind of cheer
72 Kennel sounds
73 Blunders

DOWN

1 Span. titles
2 Noted traveler
3 Morales of "La Bamba"
4 Capital on the Vistula River
5 Some movie transitions
6 Asian sash
7 Auto pioneer
8 It may foil a strike
9 Fanzine, e.g.
10 Lotion ingredient
11 Messy buildup
12 ___ bed
13 Reasons for makeups
18 Notes at the office
19 Sensitivity
24 Cabbage dish
26 Tricky curve
27 Fanzine focus
28 Good-bye
29 Jungle sounds
30 Herd
31 Old salt
32 Prevent

33 Barrel race site
34 Shellac
39 Kind of cord
41 Eliminates from, with "of"
42 Manor house estates
45 Cup handle
47 Friend of Bat and Doc
50 Only
51 Saint Lawrence, e.g.
52 Took steps

55 Flop
56 Miles away
57 Shaggy do
58 Leo, for one
60 Wise guys?
62 Mimic
63 Cold feet
64 Winds up
66 Wally of "Mr. Peepers"
67 Have dinner

55

BY JAY SULLIVAN

ACROSS

1 Listens
6 Malay peninsula native
10 Pompano relative
14 Playwright who coined the word "robot"
15 English novelist Victoria
16 Straight
17 River in the lyrics of "Shenandoah"
20 Bridge opening
21 Shoots for
22 Nev. neighbor
23 With skill
24 Proudly displays
28 Plays for a sucker
29 Allay
30 Inspire to foolish passion
35 Gooey
38 "Oklahoma!" role
39 In-basket item
40 Developer's map
41 How most acronyms are written
43 Opera villain?
47 Fed. retirement gp.
48 Controverts
49 Some dot-coms
54 For all to see
56 Long time abroad
57 One of a kind
58 Barely beat
59 The other shoe, say
60 Stack up
61 Prescribed amounts

DOWN

1 Prefix with centenary
2 Audi route
3 Foil cousin
4 Trees yielding elastic wood
5 "Never mind"
6 1971–72 TV courtroom drama
7 Kind of office
8 Arabian Nights name
9 Words spoken while shaking
10 Really put one's foot down
11 Pie part
12 Kind of surgery
13 Jupiter or Mars
18 June honorees
19 Rest of the afternoon
23 With regard to
24 Second in a series
25 Waikiki locale
26 K-Katy connection
27 Small denomination
28 Not satisfied
30 Religion since the seventh century
31 Gyrene's org.
32 Under sail
33 Fill-in

34 Those, in Toledo
36 Abided by
37 Jurassic carnivore
41 "My word!"
42 Belted
43 Last king of Troy
44 Salon coloring
45 One in charge of monk business
46 Sip

47 Affirm
49 Work on a paper, maybe
50 Resort on the lagoon of Venice
51 Béarnaise needs
52 First South Korean president
53 Regs.
55 Kind of fingerprint

56

BY DAVID J. KAHN

ACROSS

1 Cone maker
4 Jai alai catchers
10 Part of a good case
14 "Wheel of Fortune" purchase
15 Considerably reduced
16 Banned growth-retardant spray
17 Start of a quote about 37-Across's wife
20 Exam no-no
21 Exodus miracle
22 Food catcher of a sort
23 Hemingway, for one
26 Poetic nightfall
27 The lot
28 Quote, part 2
31 Emulate a dilettante
33 More than due?
34 Beauts
36 Arctic explorer John et al.
37 Speaker of the quote
40 Bone: Prefix
43 NFL Hall of Famer Hirsch
44 Go downhill fast
47 Spring sign
50 Quote, part 3
52 Tyke
53 "Cry ___ River"
55 Coming or going, e.g.
56 Pound sound
57 Pulitzer novelist Glasgow
60 "That ___ excuse"
61 End of the quote
65 "The Clan of the Cave Bear" novelist
66 "I mean ..."
67 People people: Abbr.
68 Flew
69 Destroys
70 Root cover?

DOWN

1 Ex-Majors?
2 Mistaken
3 Secure a door, maybe
4 Cleveland pro
5 Hot time in Paris
6 Fraud
7 Colosseum sight
8 United
9 High, in a way
10 Dietician's concern
11 Kasim's brother, in Persian folklore
12 1937 Garbo title role
13 High-pitched voices
18 Busy as ___
19 Carvey of comedy
24 1944 battle site
25 Tough
29 Sculptor Nadelman
30 Russian bread
32 Support of a sort

35 Part of EMS: Abbr.
37 "___ out!"
38 "The Man Who Fell to Earth" director
39 Baseballer Sandberg
40 Pontiac's followers
41 Provide extra support for
42 Liberated
44 Told to be quiet
45 "New Frontier" president
46 Support: Var.
48 Church chorus
49 Hitter of 511 home runs
51 Legal order
54 Notwithstanding that, briefly
58 Somme state
59 "___ prayer!"
62 Antiquity, old-style
63 Senior golfer Morgan
64 Sleeve opening?

57

BY PAULA GAMACHE

ACROSS
1 Words separator
6 Donations
10 Future queen, perhaps
14 Target
15 Heist objective
16 Comics canine
17 Favorite baseball mitt?
20 Vietnam ending
21 Kind of club
22 More futile
23 Tot.
25 Bit of humor
26 Street gibberish?
33 Scrap
34 Banded rock
35 Maligned, with "into"
36 Feudal subject
38 ___ Friday's: restaurant chain
39 Two-faced
40 First name in architecture
41 African expanse
43 Sign made with an upraised hand
44 Future spouse who's not undecided?
47 Old-fashioned quarrel settler
48 Belief system
49 Sea monster of myth
52 Popular
54 Ballet step
57 Arthurian path to salvation?
61 Conference opener?
62 Grimm offering
63 Buenos ___
64 One looking forward
65 Does away with
66 Engulf

DOWN
1 Decline
2 Tidy sum
3 Big name in snack food
4 Warning
5 Hot time in Le Havre
6 Code word for A
7 Deranged one
8 Calendar col.
9 Cat of music
10 With courtesy
11 Court score
12 Heir, often
13 ___-do-well
18 Repeatedly
19 Impertinence
24 Bank holding: Abbr.
25 Potter Wedgwood
26 Civil War Supreme Court Justice Robert
27 Prenatal prefix
28 Sell
29 Dark time
30 Easily duped
31 Muscular strength

32 It may be cutting
33 Designer for Jackie
37 More considerable
39 Washrooms, briefly
41 Affirm
42 "Something to Talk About" singer
45 Ponder
46 Diminish, as ability
49 Certain NCOs

50 Manitoba native
51 Third-oldest U.S. university
52 One of two?
53 Poetic tributes
55 Bat lead-in
56 Distort
58 Stumblebum
59 "Far out!"
60 Unique I.D.

58

BY LYNN LEMPEL

ACROSS
1 Works in a pen
6 Misunderstanding
10 Wit Bombeck
14 Rhinoceros relative
15 River past Orsk
16 Circuit
17 PLANE
20 "Death in Venice" novelist
21 Time to give up?
22 Pen chants
23 Tops
25 10-card winner
26 TRAIN
31 WPA promoter
34 Sarah Hughes feats
35 "The Social Contract" author
37 Fabled napper
38 Tiler's need
40 Social hour vessels
41 Neglected item
43 Pass
44 Lubbock-to-Dallas dir.
45 BUS
48 Knack
49 Comparative phrase
50 Omit in pronunciation
53 Animal lover's org.
55 Rat, in Rugby
59 TAXI

62 Round mass
63 Perp's payment
64 Danger
65 Bush alma mater
66 Well
67 Fashion

DOWN
1 Check
2 Etna flow
3 Hardly shy
4 Peaks
5 Ticket buyer's alert
6 Private students
7 Country on the Caspian
8 Speedy
9 Bug that may knock you out
10 Mischievous
11 Mottled horse
12 Feigned
13 Lummoxes
18 Radius neighbor
19 Agitates
24 Noncommittal remarks
25 Stuff
26 Lake name meaning "big water"
27 They may be made up
28 High home
29 Reykjavik coins
30 Letters of credit
31 Savage
32 Shuffle or reel
33 Ages badly
36 Summer headgear

38 Ornamental layer
39 Future fish
42 Attach, in a way
43 Nosh
46 "___ done!"
47 Ivan the Terrible, for one
48 Clay home
50 Like French toast
51 Gwen Verdon Broadway role

52 Favorite
53 Try
54 One of the Everly Brothers
56 Twisted
57 Racetrack boundary
58 Richard Petty's racing son
60 Magic org.
61 Hikes

59

BY STELLA DAILY

ACROSS

1 Tell
5 Smart group
10 Food fish
14 Diamond Head's island
15 Situated between poles
16 Big sandwich
17 Say with assurance
18 Chemist's favorite TV landlord?
20 Minor part
22 "Woe ___!"
23 Common Father's Day gift
24 Chemist's favorite antacid?
28 Conductor Abbado
31 Draft category
32 Former nuclear agcy.
33 Like a starless night
35 Some nest eggs
39 Chemist's favorite car?
44 Country runner, informally
45 City near Sacramento
46 Bend over forward
47 "Waterloo" group
51 Wedding accessories?
53 Chemist's favorite carnival ride?
57 "Norma ___"
58 Latin 101 verb
59 Egypt neighbor
63 Chemist's favorite holiday visitor?
67 Oliver's request
68 Yukon, e.g.: Abbr.
69 Direct
70 Guilty, for one
71 ___ gin fizz
72 Enthusiastic words
73 Bit of a blind

DOWN

1 First airline to offer transatlantic jet service
2 Rock that rolls?
3 "Pardon me"
4 Bedroom piece
5 Ginnie ___
6 Phone msg. detail
7 It was nothing to Nero
8 Speaks with authority
9 "... ___ are created equal"
10 Noted seashore vendor
11 Alamo competitor
12 Bandleader Shaw
13 Poor classroom participant
19 '60s Twins manager Sam
21 It may be golden
25 Benevolent
26 Team connection
27 City in SW Yemen
28 David is one
29 Salacious look

30 Part of a plot
34 Designer monogram
36 "___: My Story": C&W autobiography
37 Any minute now
38 Repairs, in a way
40 Industry authority
41 This and that
42 She played Carmela on "The Sopranos"
43 Olympic gymnast's disappointments
48 1899-1902 war participant

49 Restaurant employee
50 Make certain
52 Heavy steps
53 Worries
54 Stand in a loft
55 Like '80s fashion, say
56 Proceeds
60 Sweetie
61 Sphere of influence
62 Undiluted
64 Before, before
65 Once known as
66 Mos. and mos.

1	2	3	4		5	6	7	8	9		10	11	12	13
14					15						16			
17					18				19					
20			21			22					23			
		24		25	26				27					
28	29	30					31							
32				33		34			35	36	37	38		
39			40				41	42	43					
44					45				46					
		47	48	49	50		51		52					
53	54	55			56									
57			58				59		60	61	62			
63			64			65	66	67						
68				69				70						
71				72				73						

60

BY ROBERT H. WOLFE

ACROSS

1 Official decrees
7 Advise
11 No-goodnik
14 Expire
15 Medicinal plant
16 Inventor Whitney
17 Military search expert?
19 Great score
20 Quiets
21 Every partner
22 Cont. on the equator
25 Small fruit trees
26 Actress Ekberg
27 Buzzer
28 Org. led by Walter Reuther, 1946-70
29 Urban play area
31 Holey roll
33 Enduring
35 Not much
36 Joltless joe?
37 Leg, e.g.
40 Scheduled
42 "Ragged Dick" author
43 Bakers' implements
45 Big Ten sch.
47 "Bali ___"
48 Studied, with "over"
49 Blows away
50 Atlanta-based cable sta.
51 "What ___ For Love"
52 Gifts
55 Unburden
56 Secret language for the contrite?
60 "Bambi" character
61 Actress Lena
62 Eats at
63 "Echo Park" actress
64 Eliot title character
65 More than dislike

DOWN

1 Lapse
2 Kind of date
3 Bus. letters
4 Dove sounds
5 Melodic
6 Places for games
7 1965 unrest site
8 "That's ___!"
9 "Friends" friend
10 Court divider
11 Mall illumination?
12 One of the three Greek Furies
13 Soldier's headgear
18 Common pollen producers
21 Ultimate goal
22 Eban of Israel
23 Circus act, e.g.
24 When to honor kings?
26 ___ Meyers, first woman signed in the NBA
29 Naval force

30 Sound from Sandy
32 Worked on a paper
34 Fort Worth coll.
36 ___ Bingle: Crosby nickname
38 Intend
39 Lift rider
41 William Hurt's "Body Heat" role
42 Spartan
43 Like some churches

44 Medicine cabinet item
46 Felt
49 Helpless?
52 Cast leader?
53 In the thick of
54 Queen Mary, for one
56 Hold up
57 Dedicatory verse
58 ___ Moines
59 Body shop no.

61

BY LYNN LEMPEL

ACROSS
1 Sharp
6 "Call Me ___"
11 Disparity
14 Harry Belafonte's daughter
15 Out
16 "Yuck!"
17 Mod design for prison garb?
19 Big D.C. lobby
20 Social know-how
21 Great ___
23 Bumbler
27 One at a hitching post?
29 Serves
30 "Scent of a Woman" Oscar winner
31 Like colds
32 Tired of it all
33 Jordan's gp.
36 Canadian mountains denizens
37 Small inlets
38 Bump accidentally
39 Deluxe carrier
40 Nudged
41 Long, in a way
42 Made
44 Confuses
45 More virile
47 Nursery needs
48 Confuse
49 Miss
50 Hose part
51 Unabashed scrutiny?
58 Goof
59 Dakota home
60 Dismal turnout?
61 "Of course"
62 Sylvan deity
63 "Thank you" speaker, often

DOWN
1 Ancient Egyptian emblem
2 T'ai ___
3 Operated
4 Bug
5 Purify, perhaps
6 Drillmaster's command
7 Got off
8 Slight downturn
9 "Guys and Dolls" librettist Burrows
10 Had to look for, maybe
11 Pollution legislation?
12 Jibe
13 Stage
18 Merged news agency
22 Cape ___
23 Church areas
24 Undesirable aspects
25 Tree surgeons?
26 Leaning
27 Washed-out
28 Sorbet relatives

30 Kind of road
32 Wag
34 Barely move
35 Immeasurable depth
37 Spot for a scoop
38 Tenderhearted
40 Mass production specialists?
41 Protected area
43 Entirely
44 Five-time Wimbledon winner
45 Chatham chum
46 More than like
47 "Mad Max" villain
49 Purple Sage chronicler
52 Some like it hot
53 Inclined
54 San Diego attraction
55 Former Romanian president Iliescu
56 Paris-to-Amsterdam dir.
57 "Really!"

62

BY DENISE M. NEUENDORF

ACROSS

1 Kind of society
6 Stuff
10 Coal product
14 A lot
15 Luau dance
16 Word with lasting or loving
17 Rock-'n'-roll sharpshooter?
20 ___ green
21 It may have a code
22 Places for spirits
23 Hole card
24 Tie up
25 Sudden emissions
27 Vocations
29 On a roll
30 Dance
31 Beam
32 Intricate pattern
33 Blair of Britain
34 Rock-'n'-roll party?
38 Bamboozles
39 Mo. named for an emperor
40 "___ bet!"
41 Gives a thumbs-up to
42 Destructive compound
43 Looks
47 Gave a thumbs-down to
49 Big Green opponents
50 Wire: Abbr.
51 Swell
52 Before long
53 ___ Major
54 Rock-'n'-roll museum?
57 Ogle
58 Think of it
59 Mature
60 Whirlpool
61 Salts
62 Heavy reading?

DOWN

1 After-dinner order
2 "Gorillas in the Mist" setting
3 Less original
4 Head of France?
5 Dallas-to-Memphis dir.
6 Agitates
7 Like some notebook paper
8 "Sweet Liberty" director
9 Fannie ___
10 Cabinet wood
11 Boot, e.g.
12 Linchpin
13 Before, poetically
18 Enchanted realm
19 Lie next to
24 Give birth to
25 Hair pieces?
26 Double agent
28 Big periods
29 Tailor's concern
32 Comedian

33 Faithful
34 Purple-berried herb
35 Trapped
36 Project, with "out"
37 "My mistake"
38 Food fish
42 Driving aids
43 Hilo hellos
44 Open court
45 Swap shop transaction

46 Viewpoints
48 Creamy white
49 Participate
52 Opera in which Grace Bumbry debuted
53 Word processing command
54 Stein stuff
55 Sch. near Harvard
56 Meal starter?

63

BY MEL ROSEN

ACROSS

1 Hit, slangily
6 Ailurophobe's dread
9 Stale French bread?
14 Word sung in New Haven
15 Command posts, briefly
16 Lumberjacks' competition
17 Spasmodic
18 Diving bird
19 Superior to
20 Like mod clothes?
23 Presidential nickname
25 Tick off
26 Changes
27 Snoopy seeking talent?
31 Jetson family member
32 Flag supports
37 "Waiting for the Robert ___"
38 Arabic letters
40 Afghanistan's Tora ___ region
41 Béarnaise seasoning
43 First name in horror
44 Mansions, perhaps?
47 Blame
51 Nonwinning game line
52 Clamor
53 Reason to work out?
57 Keep one's ___ the ground
58 Gut reaction?
59 Circle lines: Abbr.
62 Used china, say
63 Caldwell from Australia
64 17th-century Mohegan leader
65 Stuck
66 Baseball Hall of Famer Roush
67 "Not really!"

DOWN

1 Vb. target
2 One not to trust
3 Sacrificing type
4 City ENE of Reno
5 Garden bloomer
6 Makes sore, in a way
7 Greenish blue
8 Reproachful sounds
9 Weakness
10 Volcano explorer, perhaps
11 "In bad company," to Ambrose Bierce
12 "You ___ know"
13 Campus figures
21 Dr. of rap
22 Tugs
23 Red as ___
24 '70s pol Abzug
28 Suffix with church
29 Its flag has five stars
30 Bumbler

33 "___ Ben Adhem"
34 Test always done in ink
35 Less lively, as prose
36 Fresh
38 Square (with)
39 Elton's john
42 Take the money and run
43 Prepared for mailing, perhaps
45 Removed
46 Prefix meaning "complete"

47 Crosswise to the keel
48 Tropical raccoon relative
49 Preserver of a kind
50 Release
54 Slime
55 Menu fare
56 Serious lapses
60 Sheepish sound
61 Jacksonville-to-St. Pete dir.

64

BY RANDALL J. HARTMAN

ACROSS

1 Totes
5 Commandment word
10 Believed
14 Words to an old man?
15 Jazz pianist Chick
16 Mayberry lad
17 Avian Getz song, with "The"?
20 Writer Hentoff
21 Beech family trees
22 Make beloved
23 Street races?
25 Hammett hound
26 Trains over the city
27 Cast member with Dick and Dan et al.
28 It's cut and dried
31 "Home ___"
34 Smudge
35 Feels poorly
36 Avian Joplin ballad?
39 Martin or Matalin
40 Big name in gossip
41 Additional
42 Agreements
43 "Confound it!"
44 ___-cone
45 Concluded
46 Smoke partner
50 Harmony
53 Kind of palm
54 Decorator's suggestion
55 Avian Gershwin tune?
58 David's father-in-law
59 Ticked
60 Oratorio segment
61 Wilson of "Raising Arizona"
62 Bred winners?
63 Education pioneer

DOWN

1 Highway aids
2 Like some suspects?
3 122-square-mile Mediterranean republic
4 One of five in "abbreviation": Abbr.
5 Hits the road
6 Angler's supply
7 Second Amendment word
8 Organic necklace
9 Woven display
10 Two-time Best Actress Oscar winner
11 Dueling sword
12 Seat of Allen County, Ohio
13 Spree
18 Duped
19 Stud fee?
24 1974 role for Dustin
25 Oranjestad's island
27 "___ Came Jones": '50s hit
28 Tipsy

29 Downwind
30 North Sea feeder
31 Fire from a heater?
32 Reporter's source
33 Henley competitors
34 Cumberland Gap explorer
35 Penn or Pitt
37 Wilson Supreme Court appointee
38 "Niagara" costar
43 Dweeb
44 Showed audible impatience

45 Embroidered ornament
46 Photo finish
47 Butler's woman
48 Altercation
49 Malibu or Park Avenue
50 Type of prof.
51 Scorch
52 Rock's Mötley ___
53 Practice on canvas
56 Canton bordering the Lake of Lucerne
57 Emeril exclamation

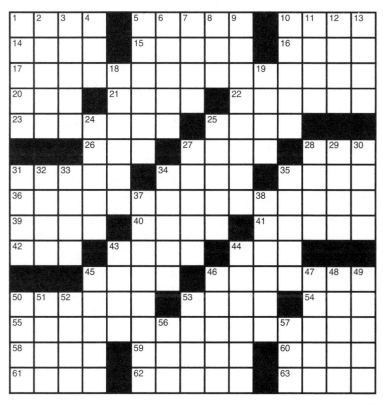

65

BY DENISE NEUENDORF

ACROSS
1 Spot
5 Heirloom locale
10 Teen hangout
14 "Growing Up in New Guinea" author
15 Horned beast
16 "The African Queen" co-screenwriter
17 1951 N.L. Rookie of the Year
18 Muhammad's birthplace
19 Chime
20 Circle segment
21 Sign of sharks near Helsinki?
23 Congo, formerly
25 Contemptible
26 Amontillado, for one
28 Menu item
30 "Two Treatises of Government" author
31 Pine Tree State
32 Freudian subject
35 Cries of wonder
36 Chop
37 Farm team
38 NBA stats
39 Squalor
40 Craft
41 Without enthusiasm

42 Show of obeisance
43 John of "Exodus"
45 Penny-pinching
46 Kin in Bangkok?
49 Peculiar
52 "The Raven" opening
53 Golfer's set
54 Circus performer?
55 Crackerjacks
56 Love
57 Boxing ringer
58 Cover, as expenses
59 Bumpkin
60 Land in water

DOWN
1 1996 Gwyneth Paltrow film
2 Cauterize
3 Wages in Prague?
4 FG units
5 Weapons source
6 "Over ___"
7 Spasms
8 Cuzco native
9 West Virginia resource
10 Fishy?
11 Getting on, so to speak
12 Pop singer Kravitz
13 Some drumsticks
21 Calamitous
22 Something to save?
24 Old flatboats
26 Spill (over)
27 Minimum of concern
28 ___ hose

134

29 Loaded
31 Move aimlessly
32 Voter surveys in Warsaw?
33 Hairdo holders
34 Nothing but
36 Earth locale
37 Gumbo vegetable
39 Impetus
40 Petitions
41 Most uninteresting

42 Swindle
43 Twist, e.g.
44 Show opener
45 Military training group
46 Pillow filler
47 Stink, so to speak
48 Pan fighter
50 Valley
51 Valley
54 It has an academy in Quantico, Va.

66

BY PAULA GAMACHE

ACROSS

1 Aspen merchandise
7 Airheads
15 State categorically
16 Save time at the hospital, maybe
17 Mugger's demand
19 Sports lover's choice
20 Disintegrates
21 Tear apart
22 Some Caltech grads
23 Cookie holder
26 Beginning of victim's response
33 Staves off
34 Certain soup contents
37 Classic grape soda
38 Remove using force
39 Revolutionary War hero Warner
40 Busted, so to speak
43 Lighter fuel
45 End of victim's response
47 Keeper's charge
48 Corrida cheer
49 Bellow
53 Riskily off base
55 Jumbo, for one
59 Mugger's new demand
63 Reached the peak
64 Plate watcher
65 Rationality
66 Basil-based sauces

DOWN

1 Beep
2 Sale notation
3 Request to an invitee
4 Sharp
5 Extension
6 Den setups
7 Pooch in a primer
8 How a curmudgeon might speak
9 Woman, objectively
10 Battlefield for many a vet
11 Secret target?
12 Potent opening
13 Capital on the Dnieper River
14 Eye infection
18 Eddie of the '40s-'50s Senators
22 N.J. summer hrs.
24 AOL, e.g.
25 Fed. med. research agency
26 Andrews of "Laura"
27 In excess of
28 ___ jacket: '60s fad
29 Takes a shot at
30 Georgia doesn't have one
31 Baltimore clipper's pair
32 Crosswise, nautically

35 Europe's highest
   volcano
36 Consequential word
38 Some aliases
41 Fi lead-in
42 Significant amount
43 Out of business
44 Purpose
46 Maneuverer's need
49 "Arabian Nights" birds
50 Norman's home: Abbr.

51 Not fer
52 Hoarfrost
54 Joins together
55 Bribes
56 Part of an OK,
   perhaps
57 Losing score
58 Watchers
60 Relocating aid
61 River in Devonshire
62 Marseille Mrs.

67

BY ED EARLY

ACROSS

1 Island off Tuscany
5 Pouches
9 Part of a calyx
14 Cover, as a room
15 Arthur Ashe's alma mater
16 Living
17 Convention site
18 Dump closure?
19 Relieved
20 Start of a quip
23 Nice hot time
24 Clears
25 Met expectations?
28 Ram maker
30 "Ain't We Got Fun" lyricist Kahn
31 Fifth in N.Y.C., e.g.
32 Where to get in line?
34 Dress (up)
35 Pass over
36 Part 2 of the quip
41 In the old days
42 NASA thumbs-up
43 Links support
44 Schedule abbr.
45 Yell
46 Words to an audience
50 Military helmet
52 "Wait ___!"
55 The Silver St.
56 End of the quip
59 Vin choice
61 Vaunt
62 Not quite closed
63 Northampton college
64 Gutter locale
65 Tirade
66 Like a bundle of nerves
67 Strategic WWI river
68 Lbs. and oz.

DOWN

1 Repeated
2 Shed with a single-pitch roof
3 Formally charged
4 Associate
5 Bite-sized dish
6 Performed
7 Staff figures
8 Over-the-shoulder garment
9 Saturates
10 Make disappear
11 Deli order
12 Dog-days drink
13 Was ahead
21 Nottingham's river
22 Nutty confection
26 See 58-Down
27 Clockmaker Thomas
29 Former heavyweight champ Tunney
30 Jesse Ventura, once: Abbr.

33 Shortage
34 "Mustn't do that"
35 Low digits
36 Epic creator
37 Protester
38 "No rush"
39 Three-time Vezina Trophy winner Patrick
40 Give feedback
45 Easily hummable
47 Fixed, so to speak
48 Do a sommelier's job
49 Turns inside out
51 Clues
52 Kirlian photography images
53 Barrel element
54 Raring to go
57 Follow
58 With 26-Down, curiosity
59 Org. with Cubs and Eagles
60 K-O connection

68

BY DAVID J. KAHN

ACROSS
1 Conestoga, for one
6 Vietnam fighters
10 High coif
14 Skip the formalities, in a way
15 Shaft entrance
16 Holm oak
17 Druggist-turned-movie star?
20 "Super, man!"
21 Behind the eight ball
22 Class action gp.?
23 Masseuse's target
25 Butcher's cuts
26 ___ alai
27 Use well
29 1990 World Series champs
30 Each, in scores
31 Dazzled
32 Computer attachment?
33 "Gunsmoke" role
35 Runs through
36 Bracelet site
39 Word uttered while shaking one's head
40 Flier to Oslo
43 Finicky kid in a Life cereal ad
44 Printemps follower
46 Bombard

47 "Cape Fear" actor
48 Subsidy
49 Yemen's locale
51 Worthless
52 Walton of Wal-Mart
53 Weasel cousin
55 "... but for the grace of God ___"
56 Inventor-turned-movie star?
59 Netting
60 Aware of
61 Western scene
62 Applies
63 An ex of Madonna
64 Office solution

DOWN
1 Play Washington, say
2 "Any Given Sunday" actor
3 Philanthropist-turned-TV personality?
4 Show a preference
5 "M*A*S*H" soda
6 Ghoulish
7 Some potatoes
8 Bordeaux's department
9 Dos
10 Display
11 Short-order-cook-turned-TV personality?
12 Alamo offering
13 Beefy stew ingredient
18 Tolkien creature
19 Some toasters

24 Cary of "Glory"
28 Blotter site
33 "___ the torpedoes!": Farragut
34 Tear jerker?
37 Freed
38 Cosmetics item
40 Main route?
41 Lake Louise locale
42 Many a nametag

44 "Chico and the Man" setting
45 Glinting toppers
46 Ad agency strategies
49 Galoot
50 High-wire-act response
54 Finesse
57 Molière's "L'école ___ femmes"
58 Letter after pi

69

BY LEONARD WILLIAMS

ACROSS
1 Garden lure
6 Rhodes with a scholarship
11 Unwinding locale
14 Group with a plot
15 Consequently
17 Start of a quip
19 ___ XING
20 Nights before
21 Leontyne Price role
22 Notion
24 NBA Hall of Famer Greer
26 Quip, part 2
33 "Sweet and Lowdown" director
34 Worry
35 Elementary suffix
37 Elementary gp., perhaps
38 Similar
40 Old Pontiac
41 Some coll. students
42 "La Vie en Rose" singer
43 Bangkok bread
45 Quip, part 3
49 Batik need
50 It's at home on the range
51 Delirious
54 Polite address
56 Machu Picchu resident

60 Speaker of the quip
64 Good point
65 Brings to tears?
66 Piglet pal
67 Cube, for one
68 Top

DOWN
1 Sarcastic
2 Hustle
3 Slender reed
4 Composer Ravel
5 The whole enchilada
6 Oil site
7 Ferrara ruling family
8 Raven's cries
9 Nest egg segment
10 Draped greeting
11 Mystical Muslim
12 Walk heavily
13 Gillette brand
16 Trite
18 GPA reducers, probably
23 Home room
24 Take on
25 Stun
26 Patsies
27 Extremist
28 Not blend
29 Bradbury genre
30 Sturdy wood
31 Stars' showcase?
32 All, in music
36 Very
38 Helper on the Hill

39 Field with cases
42 Type of envelope
43 Bx. or Bklyn.
44 Accountant, at times
46 Mystery writers' award
47 Became less aloof
48 Spheric opening
51 Nearly shut
52 Head for
53 Able to see through

54 Handle roughly
55 Foe
57 Irresponsible emperor
58 Sailors
59 Org.
61 "___ folly to be wise": Gray
62 "Six Feet Under" network
63 Comcast subsidiary

70

BY EDWARD W. KARASEK

ACROSS
1 View from Guantánamo Bay
5 Knight's neighbor
11 Chalet backdrop
14 Change for a tip, maybe
15 Mall feature
16 Call from the stands
17 First-quarter-moon tide
18 "Vanessa" composer Samuel
19 Blubber
20 Search for one's roots?
22 Gives birth to
23 Erie Canal city
24 ___-relief
25 Rodolfo's love, in "La Bohème"
26 D.C. century
27 Altar ego?
30 Devilish
32 Bath site: Abbr.
33 Piglet's pal
35 Incites
36 Municipal paper supply?
39 Washington neighbor
42 Pelt
43 Old man
46 No longer in use
49 Roxy Music cofounder
50 One of the Gabors

51 They keep you from passing
52 Surprised cries
54 Prefer
56 "Float like a butterfly" boxer
57 Mallards' wake-up call?
60 Greatest degree
61 Elevated
62 Toward the calm side
63 Nice season
64 Put in a row
65 Smooth idle
66 Video game letters
67 Alternatives to purchases
68 Hardy character

DOWN
1 Nonplus
2 Still on the plate
3 Cheerful
4 Savory gelatin
5 Coddle
6 Desert Storm target
7 Clean with effort
8 ___ corpus
9 Black Sea port
10 Saucy
11 Curved
12 Fort on the Oregon Trail
13 Foucault's field
21 Parody
25 Lunar plain
28 Seating arrangement

144

29 Rob Reiner, to Carl
31 Highway exit
34 Operations ctrs.
36 Like so
37 Four-stringed instrument
38 "Am ___ time?"
39 Madison Avenue types
40 Let some air out of
41 Tacks on

43 Cheapen
44 Staunch advocates
45 Sewers, at times
47 One might be an item
48 Muse of comedy
53 Some medical tests
55 Get to fit
57 Kind of control: Abbr.
58 Where breeches end
59 Likelihood

71

BY LOUIS HILDEBRAND

ACROSS
1 Cool drink
5 Dastardly
9 Luxurious fur
14 Is worth it
15 Towel brand
16 Polk's predecessor
17 Start of a question to a grocery clerk
20 Ancient character
21 Polite address
22 Brownies' org. until 1947
23 End of the question
26 Prominent print
27 Vessel designation
28 Take from
29 "Los Caprichos" painter
31 Had a passion (for)
33 New Haven collegians
35 Melodic
37 Start of the clerk's answer
42 Waver
43 Like some history
45 It's hard to read
48 Ill-considered
51 Rage
52 Quebec's ___ d'Orléans
53 ___ dog
55 Answer, part 2
57 Sea shocker
58 Hardly a big wheel
59 Shoe polish brand
60 End of the answer
66 Forest obscurers?
67 Fertilizer material
68 Tiny bit
69 Tact, for example
70 Sharon's "Cagney & Lacey" costar
71 Berserk

DOWN
1 Bad Ems, for one
2 It may be in a lock
3 Work on roots, perhaps
4 Rusty Staub, once
5 Be that as it may
6 Holding gadget
7 "Now ___ seen everything!"
8 It may have a noose
9 Hoagy Carmichael standard
10 "Atlas Shrugged" author Rand
11 Ruin
12 Flat dweller
13 Adenauer's successor
18 Like some juries
19 Bolster
23 Vein find
24 ___ me tangere
25 Footnote abbr.
26 Heart transplant pioneer
30 Chatters

32 Area below Greenwich Village
34 1998 N.L. MVP
36 "The Music Man" setting
38 Anchor venue
39 Betray, kid-style
40 Sandusky's lake
41 Tall tale
44 Judge's decision
45 Nap
46 Proves innocent
47 Depends (on)

49 Muslim fundamentalist
50 Benjamin portrayer
54 Camp David Accords participant
56 Watchfulness
59 Aga ___
61 Aberdeen's river
62 Mystery writer Josephine
63 ___-hoo
64 Series ender
65 Confucian path

72

BY DENISE M. NEUENDORF

ACROSS
1 Sky light
5 Verbal nudge
9 Bother
14 First name in folk
15 Really excite
16 Trendy '80s color
17 Outspoken Indochina residents?
19 Carol musician
20 Hypothetical portal
21 Snow White's Dwarfs, e.g.
22 Rather field
23 Needlefish
24 Bar order
25 Montana city
28 Birch family trees
30 Simple card game
31 Like many salads
34 Muse group
37 Leftover piece
39 Two-ton beast
40 Elderly
41 Stress-reducing discipline
42 Peals
44 Witchy woman
45 E-mail connection?
47 Like many bad decisions
49 Batting stat: Abbr.
51 Tear

52 Lady Macbeth concern
54 Plastered
56 "The Merry Widow," e.g.
60 Packing aid
61 Affirmative hisses?
62 Amber, for one
63 Zoning unit
64 Lose it
65 "Awake and Sing!" dramatist
66 Driving aids
67 Fish usually lacking a tail fin

DOWN
1 Season, in a way
2 "Star Trek: The Next Generation" counselor
3 School supporter, often
4 Beaver, e.g.
5 "Baloney!"
6 Brands, maybe
7 Quick cut
8 NFL scores
9 One facing the pitcher
10 Annoyance
11 Big shows of relief?
12 "___ Day": Holly hit
13 To the point
18 Bird call
21 Bogie's "High Sierra" role
23 Friendship 7 astronaut
25 Body type?
26 Biblical preposition

27 Hard-nosed act?
28 Indian, say
29 Genetic material
32 Common corsage
33 Tote: Var.
35 Nifty
36 Having butterflies
38 Howl
43 Vacation spot
46 Smooths ruffled feathers
48 Military command

49 Minute Maid Park player
50 Swore
52 Flat substitute
53 Some lap dogs, briefly
55 Distraught state
56 It may be enough
57 Actress Daly
58 Pond swimmer
59 Feared snakes
61 Posed

73

BY CATHY MILLHAUSER

ACROSS
1 Male swans
5 Magician James
10 Tent event
14 Iris locale
15 Swell place?
16 Cereal with a spokesrabbit
17 Kid's meal vegetable?
19 Griddle-baked Indian bread
20 Binging
21 Place after the Pennsylvania Railroad?
23 Los ___: city near San Jose
25 Genre of Escher's "Relativity"
26 Couldn't sleep ___
29 Uses the microwave, perhaps
32 Kid's meal bread?
35 Unmatched
38 Personal
39 Sheepish
40 Pair
41 When doubled, a Gabor
42 Kid's meal entrée?
45 Trumpet sound
46 Shoat's quotes
47 ___ glasses
50 Leveling wedges
53 Its top speed is about 70 mph
56 Efficient, as a floor-care product
60 Rent
61 Kid's meal dessert?
63 Geraint's wife
64 Quick
65 Ruby and garnet
66 Supports in the ground
67 "I heard you"
68 Once, once

DOWN
1 King work
2 It may be Dutch
3 Composer Bartók
4 Leaping
5 Metal worker?
6 Vinegary prefix
7 Federal cultural funding gp.
8 Rather and more
9 Scientific org.
10 Backpack features
11 Pizzeria output
12 Carafe, often
13 Have a life
18 Omelet maker's discards, perhaps
22 Cheek
24 Advances
26 Complete range
27 Blows away
28 Isle of Mull neighbor

30 Hägar the Horrible's daughter
31 Round in a pub
33 Buffalo Bill's birthplace
34 At any time
35 Frigg's husband, in Norse myth
36 Gloaming
37 "The Simpsons" cries
42 Saloon door piece
43 Big hit
44 Narrow opening
45 Fosters
47 Quarts in a peck, e.g.
48 Word with tag or home
49 Chilling
51 Big name in games
52 Suggest
54 Barely open
55 Former Justice Black
57 Half a cake, maybe
58 LAX postings
59 "Yo!" quietly
62 Saw guide

74

BY ROBERT H. WOLFE

ACROSS

1 Comic work, perhaps
6 Crab's sensor
10 Actress Sue ___ Langdon
13 Purity unit
14 "___ of the Mind": Shepard play
15 Newspaper page
16 Antioxidant?
18 Campbell of "Party of Five"
19 Supermodel Carol
20 Records
21 Some feds
22 One of the British?
23 Basketry raw materials
25 Layers
28 Art of film
30 Earth
31 Fictional detective
33 Put together again, in a way
36 Onetime White House briefing name
37 Starts a hole, and title of this puzzle
39 Versatile wheels
40 "One Million Years B.C." actress
42 Lyrical nights
43 "East of Eden" son
44 Prepares chicken Kiev
46 Remnant
48 Expands
50 Cyborg movie prefix
51 Pointer's pronoun
52 Deceptions
55 Trickery
58 Tear down
59 Hatchet man?
61 Manipulative sort
62 Babbles
63 Reunion attendee
64 View from Toulon
65 Hook's mate
66 Do a salon job

DOWN

1 Stew vegetable
2 Composer Dukas
3 Formerly, formerly
4 Scoundrel
5 Maximally
6 Stick together
7 Der ___: Adenauer
8 Recumbent one
9 Individual
10 Kong's height, e.g.?
11 Defiant response
12 Perfect spots
15 Prompt
17 Prepare to remove, maybe
22 "Who ___": Jessica Andrews hit
24 Lowly worker
25 Popular side

26 Sped
27 Amtrak employee's jacket?
28 Quantity buys
29 Aware of
32 Consider
34 School founded by Henry VI
35 Proceed
37 "___ Came to Cordura": 1959 film
38 Shooters' considerations
41 Big depression

43 Past
45 Analyzes
47 Away
48 Play lightly
49 Something to go through
50 Charlotte ___
53 Final
54 Capture
55 On the main
56 Legendary birds
57 Trunk site
60 You across the Atlantic

75

BY DAVID AINSLIE
MACLEOD

ACROSS

1 Blue cheese alternative
8 Minimally
15 Seaweed eater
16 With 65-Across, puzzle title suggested by the ends of 4-, 23-, and 24-Down
17 ___ Beach: L.A. suburb
18 Had a sandwich, perhaps
19 Mustang ancestor
20 Web address suffix
21 Also
22 Prohibit
23 Suit material
25 Musical with the song "Bosom Buddies"
28 Also
30 Sneakily involve
34 Man ___: 1920 Triple Crown contender
35 Shrine Game team
37 Skating medalist Slutskaya
38 Silky synthetic
40 Literary monogram
41 Zhou ___
42 Brigham Young University site
43 Ship's pole

45 Actress Best
46 Attachment adverb
48 Pay dirt
49 Exploit
50 Charged
52 Half a cocktail
54 Bustle
57 Pro ___
58 Shoots the breeze
62 Shaw play
64 Occasionally
65 See 16-Across
66 Farm machines
67 Ancient Palestinians
68 Color-codes, e.g.

DOWN

1 ___ avis
2 Over in Germany
3 Thompson of "Family"
4 Get mawkish with
5 Ancient Aegean area
6 Slow movement
7 Broadway brightener
8 Beaming
9 Traveled, in a way
10 It may be sexy
11 Business letter abbr.
12 Mohammad Khan, for one
13 WWII gun
14 White House maiden name
23 One who can't pass the bar?

24 Half of a no-win comment
25 Change, in sci-fi flicks
26 Mindful
27 Local boss
29 Important grain
31 "Lady Windermere's Fan" playwright
32 Silly
33 River nymph
36 Emotional flower?
39 Marginal reference
44 Den gadgets
47 Antsy
51 Stockpile
53 Gets the kitty going
54 Entr'___
55 Morse code tones
56 People
58 Home in Durango
59 Part of AFL-CIO: Abbr.
60 "Mary Poppins" chimney sweep
61 Snake's warning
63 AES defeater

76

BY DENISE M. NEUENDORF

ACROSS

1 Expletive eraser
6 "___! I've Said It Again": old #1 hit
11 Mini, maybe
14 Rush site
15 More inexperienced
16 It may be bruised
17 Definition of "consultant," part 1
19 Sign of summer
20 Move ashamedly
21 Heirs, often
22 Concords
26 Quick on the uptake
28 Definition, part 2
31 Spaces
32 Started to smoke
33 Cauldron stirrers
34 Dutch cheese
36 General Bradley
40 Standing tall
42 Chilling
43 Definition, part 3
46 Dark
48 Most adroit
49 Boccie battlefield
50 Common chord
52 Part of AST: Abbr.
53 End of definition
59 Roller that isn't round

60 "Hawaii Five-O" detective, to his boss
61 Fluctuates
62 Last word?
63 Yarn unit
64 Gustavus V, for one

DOWN

1 Yuppie purchase, perhaps
2 ___-di-dah
3 Historic period
4 Braggart's suffix
5 Field in which fields are studied
6 It's obvious
7 1944 chemistry Nobelist Otto
8 Furry ally of Han and Leia
9 Sell (for)
10 Before, to Byron
11 Upholstery fabric
12 Star's go-between
13 Oater omen
18 Stick in the fridge
21 Command to a hack
22 Bountiful locale
23 Romance novelist Roberts
24 "___ your indulgence"
25 Table setting item
26 Old Spice alternative
27 R-V hookup?
29 Get by
30 Support

34 Like some R-rated films
35 Unsafe?
37 Bog down
38 Links feats
39 Musical symbol
41 Mai tai ingredient
42 Unproductive periods
43 Wailed
44 Kinetoscope inventor
45 Biweekly tide
46 Forest clearing

47 Pig ___
50 Melody
51 Indian royalty
53 NFL stats
54 Hard wood
55 Start of a popular round
56 Storm feature
57 Agree, in a way
58 "The Waste Land" poet's monogram

77

BY BARBARA OLSON

ACROSS

1 Features of 20-, 33-, 42-, and 57-Across
5 Wore
10 Precise location
14 Linear calculation
15 "I was asleep," for one
16 Himalayan legend
17 Knickknack site, maybe
18 Blemish
19 Light gas
20 New office placements
23 Varnish resin
24 Hairy-ape link
25 Pretend to be
27 Georgia, once: Abbr.
28 Itinerary letters
31 Not allowed
33 Dipped appetizer
37 Nobel Peace Prize presentation site
40 Prepare
41 Homer Simpson's hangout
42 "Luck Be a Lady" musical
45 Stage deliveries
46 Stutz contemporary
47 One-time link
50 Space-saving abbr.
51 1965 NCAA tennis champ

55 Old Italian bread?
57 Butchers' aids
61 Paramount
62 Sleep disorder
63 Cry from a slide
64 Ain't right?
65 Goes around
66 Snobby quality
67 Denmark-based building company
68 Law recipient
69 Capone nemesis

DOWN

1 Personal preferences
2 Cantilevered windows
3 Disciplinarian, perhaps
4 Home of Willamette University
5 Leftovers dish
6 Quartet member
7 Roman goddess of the hunt
8 Awards since 1956
9 Ancient mercenary
10 Harmony
11 Sheer, as a blouse
12 Canal examiner's aid
13 Its symbol is Sn
21 Fishing locale
22 Not backing
26 Throw
29 Needing stitches
30 Got 10 out of 10 on, say
32 They can help if you're short

158

33 Big name in stereo components
34 Rogue
35 Baking soda target
36 Talbot of "Ozzie & Harriet"
37 Stare at
38 Carousel rider?
39 Oater justice, maybe
43 Urgent letters
44 Relax on the sofa

47 Friend of Jughead
48 Willing souls
49 Estimate formally
52 Tic
53 Veld grazer
54 Capital of County Clare
56 Hoover, for one
58 Not fooled by
59 Actor Hackman
60 Quartet member
61 Wire measure

78

BY ALAN ARBESFELD

ACROSS

1 Overworked mgr.'s need
5 Eban of Israel
9 Strong
14 A son of Adam
15 Benefit
16 "Turandot," for one
17 About, contractually
18 Left at sea
19 Heep of "David Copperfield"
20 False
23 Spanish philosopher José ___ y Gasset
24 NRC predecessor
25 Good discount, e.g.
32 "Leaving on ___ Plane"
35 Story
36 Lab burners
37 Airline with the subsidiary Linjeflyg
38 Absolutely on target
40 Hint
41 Stunned
43 Beef order
44 D.C. denizens
45 Red, for one
48 Furthermore
49 Weather Channel subject
53 Forward-looking system
58 "___ card, any card"
59 Another, in Madrid
60 Indian tourist city
61 Sheer
62 Fontanne of Broadway
63 Insubstantial
64 Word needed to complete this puzzle's theme
65 Cans
66 Letters from Greece

DOWN

1 "... say, and not ___"
2 Title for Cervantes
3 Self-important gait
4 Top-notch
5 Interest
6 Coalition
7 Gore Vidal historical novel
8 Respecting
9 Dog, perhaps
10 Brandy flavoring
11 Control
12 Elapse tediously
13 Impatient cry
21 Shirt size: Abbr.
22 Bend under pressure
26 King of talk
27 Kind of artery
28 River to the Amazon
29 A big fan of
30 Execute perfectly, in slang
31 Recipe amts.
32 Pronto

33 Five-time NHL scoring leader Jaromir
34 Actor Morales
38 Toledo resident
39 Military band tubas
42 Simoleon
44 Allot according to ownership
46 Nutrition inits.
47 Big Ten sch.
50 Gulf
51 Mall features
52 "___ Daughter": 1970 film
53 In ___: unmoved
54 Hepta- plus one
55 "Damn Yankees" vamp
56 Group with the 1979 #1 hit "Babe"
57 Coastal flier
58 Curly-tailed dog

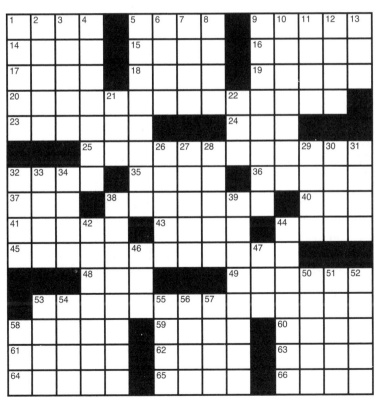

79

BY DENISE M. NEUENDORF

ACROSS

1 Cowboy, at times
6 Novelist Genet
10 Casa cookware
14 Pop up
15 Brontë orphan
16 Diving bird
17 They're saved for rainy days
18 Start of a quote
20 Greek vowel
21 News agcy. since '58
23 Visits
24 With 38-Down, high-tech ending
25 Have trouble with sassafras?
27 Indignation
28 Quote, part 2
34 Cubs' gp.
35 Big blow
36 Draw upon
37 Flu symptom
40 Shells, maybe
42 Whirled
43 Deer mom
44 Enjoy the sun
45 "I told you so!"
47 Quote, part 3
53 Scooby-___
54 Breakfast area
55 "Read Across America" sponsor: Abbr.
56 Smart comments
60 Traffic court letters
61 Coffee hour need
62 End of the quote
64 Folkways
66 Sample
67 Nike competitor
68 Past plump
69 Fill completely
70 Removable cover
71 Fiber used in rug-making

DOWN

1 Fit for everyone
2 Figure of speech?
3 Freebooter
4 "The Reach of the Mind" subject
5 Sports page listings
6 Kind of calendar
7 Looker
8 C's, for instance
9 Shipshape
10 One who knows the ropes
11 "Relax!"
12 Burt's ex
13 Not just yet
19 Urban polluter
22 Beating sound
26 Leather source
29 Grandpa Simpson
30 First name in slavery

31 City on the Clyde
32 Fighting Tigers' sch.
33 Urge
37 Classified info?
38 See 24-Across
39 Driver's protection
41 Blond shade
42 Stitch
44 Cause to swell
46 Northern people, historically
48 Track down
49 Words spoken before walking out
50 Toughens
51 Mother quoted in this puzzle
52 Fairy tale brother
56 Some drillers: Abbr.
57 Neck of the woods
58 Smack
59 Relocate
63 Compete
65 Tie in the East

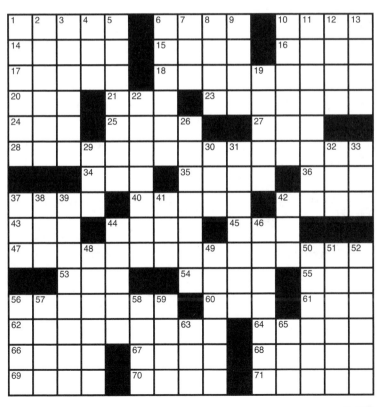

80

BY BARBARA OLSON

ACROSS
1 Like the shipwrecked Robinsons
6 End
10 Captain Kirk adversary
14 Snap
15 1991 Pulitzer poet Van Duyn
16 Incantation opener
17 Send everyone home
19 ___ Blanc: Michigan resort island
20 Uruguay city
21 Foot part
22 Ajax rival
23 Celebrate, in a way
26 Elegantly lithe
29 Impediments
30 Sea wall relative
31 Cell, maybe
33 Tangle
36 Slightly
37 Word missing from 17-, 23-, 44-, and 56-Across
38 Diminish
39 When repeated, a confection
40 More than ask
41 Loud, to Liszt
42 When repeated, a Jim Carrey movie
43 Look, slangily
44 Burglarize
49 "Uh uh!"
50 Camp sacks?
51 Victor's wife, in "Casablanca"
55 Do
56 Start a quick getaway
58 Green Gables girl
59 Celtic tongue
60 Erupt, as tempers
61 Psychic
62 River through Hesse
63 Circus sights

DOWN
1 Soap residue
2 Paper towel, e.g.
3 Like JFK and LAX
4 Taught
5 Dockside pronoun
6 Savvy
7 Fire illegally
8 Traveling
9 Use plastic, say
10 Skewered servings
11 Subject of a '52 test
12 The Little Mermaid
13 Mean-spirited
18 Cracker topper
22 Freezer unit
24 Eponymous Beehive State tribe
25 Hogwash
26 No small piece
27 Nix

164

28 "Mrs. Bridge" novelist Connell
31 Prepare to air later
32 "Isn't ___ bit like you and me?": Beatles lyric
33 Hospital section
34 Major ending?
35 Stout cousin
37 Dull
38 Really lazy
40 Compassion
41 Followers of mis

42 Layabout
43 Overflow
44 Conquistador victims
45 Not a soul
46 Packing rope
47 Kid (around)
48 Mud-sliding mammal
52 Car buyer's aid
53 Prepare laundry, maybe
54 Bellicose god
56 Charge
57 Young newt

1	2	3	4	5		6	7	8	9		10	11	12	13
14						15					16			
17				18							19			
20					21					22				
			23	24				25						
26	27	28					29							
30					31	32				33	34	35		
36				37					38					
39			40				41							
		42					43							
44	45	46				47	48							
49				50				51	52	53	54			
55			56			57								
58			59			60								
61			62			63								

81

BY ALAN ARBESFELD

ACROSS
1 Chats
5 Bother in kindergarten
9 Peddles
14 Major
15 Bumpkin
16 Waters of blues
17 Do some casting
18 ___ impulse
19 Love abroad
20 Upset, in the barnyard?
23 Former California fort
24 Mass. summer hours
25 Hosted
27 Promotional assortment
31 Shock
34 Skip the reception?
35 Chevron rival
38 Military group
39 Jeff Lynne's rock gp.
40 Colorful bands
43 Make sure of
44 Work on the road
46 Actress Falco
47 Arch lead-in
49 Third Reich chronicler William
51 Expects
53 Soft coat
56 Soldier, perhaps
57 Knock

59 Sorcery, in the barnyard?
64 Big name in chips
66 "Lady Jane Grey" playwright
67 '50s–'60s singer of many a request
68 Alarming situation
69 Family group
70 Shah's land, once
71 Muslim palace area
72 On its way
73 Knock out

DOWN
1 Bridges in films
2 "... baked in ___ "
3 Big name in chips
4 Lug: Var.
5 Yorkshire literary name
6 Hierarchy level
7 Like ___ in the woods
8 Popular break time, briefly
9 Hamm shot
10 Withdrawal site
11 Mysteries, in the barnyard?
12 Drama critic Walter
13 Travel aided by runners
21 Runs without moving
22 One expecting a hand, perhaps
26 Nice water
27 Runs very slowly
28 God of the Koran

29 Celebrity, in the barnyard?
30 Grass stalk
32 Tiny
33 Had leftovers, say
36 Lab subj.
37 Help on the way up
41 Jeopardy
42 Range name
45 Go awry
48 Heartburn remedy
50 Symbol

52 Feel sorry about
54 Bust makers
55 Where élèves congregate
57 Antenna type
58 Huáscar subject
60 2002 skating bronze medalist
61 Bush battler
62 Eye-catching Apple
63 Rap on the head
65 Afore

82

BY CASEY PUTWORTH

ACROSS

1 With 29-Across, time to avoid 67-Across
7 One of the 67-Across
15 Belgrade's river
16 Rising notes?
17 11th-century Italian theologian
18 Parsley family herb
19 Chukka boot fabrics
21 Metz moniker
22 Where-at link
25 ___-Cat
26 Early 35mm cameras
29 See 1-Across
33 Short lab worker?
34 Caper
35 Acts unpredictably, as a stock price
37 Island strings
38 Abu ___
42 "Wide World of Sports" creator Arledge
44 Teacher's handout
45 With 68-Across, one of the 67-Across
49 Cajoled
51 Fed. air-quality watchdog
52 Mother's group?
53 Actress MacGraw
54 Eventually float to shore
57 Vietnam patrol boat
61 Cancún, for one
65 "Aha!"
66 Sobieski of "Joan of Arc"
67 7-Across and 45-/68-Across, e.g.
68 See 45-Across

DOWN

1 Govt. product-testing org.
2 Took off
3 Pols with jobs
4 Member's payment
5 Embarrassed, maybe
6 Saudi's neighbor
7 Highlands hill
8 Cap site
9 Mean in math class: Abbr.
10 Fair in math class?
11 About .62 mi.
12 Boxing strategy
13 Reynolds Wrap's parent compnay
14 Saints and Angels
20 "Le Coq ___": 1909 opera
22 ___-bitty
23 Logical beginning?
24 Board meeting VIP
26 Permit
27 Seat of Garfield County, Oklahoma
28 Provoked scratching

168

30 Chest
31 Reserved, in a way
32 Boise-to-Bozeman dir.
36 Unique
37 Half of bi-
39 Fired
40 Naked
41 "___ old cowhand ..."
43 Signed off on
45 Gave up
46 Some TVs
47 Grueling
48 Queasy feeling

49 Tribe for whom a sea is named
50 Three-time A.L. batting champ
54 Farmer's cart
55 Courtroom figs.
56 Begged
58 It may need massaging
59 CD-___
60 Numbered rd.
62 Munic. legislator
63 Formerly named
64 "___ Rosenkavalier"

83

BY BARRY TUNICK

ACROSS
1 "By Jove!"
5 Fall guy?
9 Speeder spotter
14 Not
15 "David Copperfield" character
16 Spin doctor's concern
17 They may be thrown for a loss
18 Shades
19 Soft palate
20 Bach, Beethoven, and Brahms's queens?
23 Sculptures, e.g.
24 Support system?
25 ___ American
29 JFK and RFK
31 Like steak tartare
34 Tickle
35 Consider
36 Flu fighters
37 Israel's Netanyahu's gift radios?
40 Change for a five
41 Banjoist Scruggs
42 New Jersey's ___ Hall University
43 Builder's asset?
44 Workers on a farm
45 Catalog
46 Orbit bit
47 Bearded beast
48 Navy builders' flycatchers?
56 Try to pass the bar?
57 You saw it
58 Think piece?
60 "It's been ___ pleasure"
61 Semicircular recess
62 "Saving Private Ryan" event
63 Needing kneading, maybe
64 Takes home
65 End of a January 1 lyric

DOWN
1 Word after living or dead
2 Trot, for one
3 Flatfoot's lack
4 One in a colorful business?
5 Stick
6 Have reservations about
7 Son of Hera
8 Sunday ceremony
9 Afton and Avon
10 It multiplies by dividing
11 Broad valley
12 Fluish fit
13 Radiation measures
21 Icicle sites
22 Cold War concern
25 One with power and influence
26 Acid type

27 Enjoyed the rapids
28 Osiris's sis
29 Cold drafts
30 It holds the line
31 Odd-numbered page
32 Shady nook
33 "Fuzzy Wuzzy ___ fuzzy ..."
35 "Oh, fudge!"
36 Keeps company with
38 Picket line?
39 Give out
44 Biological ring of color

45 Battery terminals
46 Statesman Eban and others
47 Semblance
48 Bed board
49 Word on Irish coins
50 Revival meeting cry
51 Former cygnet
52 Innocent, for one
53 Contractors' offers
54 Countercurrent
55 Rap mogul Combs
59 Ahab's affirmative

84

BY MICHAEL VUOLO

ACROSS

1 Like many a horse
5 Son, in Somme
9 Grimy layer
13 Run well
14 "... like it ___!"
15 "West Side Story" role
16 Israel's '40s–'50s U.N. ambassador
17 Guitarist Eddy
18 Inventing middle name
19 Ideally
22 ___ Kan: pet food brand
23 Adlai's running mate
24 Allure
25 Hurry
27 Hurry
29 Actress/singer Zadora
30 C follower?
32 Parks on a bus
33 It may involve sin: Abbr.
34 Ideally
38 1969 Peace Prize recipient: Abbr.
39 Resourcefulness
40 Topsy's friend, in "Uncle Tom's Cabin"
41 Back talk
42 "... ___ time to do't": Lady Macbeth
43 Faith of more than one billion
47 End of an old French cheer
49 Like, and then some
53 With 58-Across, dinner option
54 Ideally
57 Dandy accessory
58 See 53-Across
59 ___ Bay: Manhattan neighborhood
60 "Bring ___!"
61 Zeniths
62 Like condors
63 Hardy heroine
64 M.D.'s order
65 Loads

DOWN

1 Converses
2 Decorative cover
3 Delphic shrine
4 Bond opponent
5 Result
6 Mindless
7 Unlikely champion
8 Editor's mark
9 Bacteria genus, briefly
10 Give way
11 Consistent
12 Its capital was Yangon
14 Track numbers
20 Pee-wee Herman trademark

21 Vacation home selling point
26 Humanities subj.
28 Accommodating comment
31 Early fifth-century date
32 Hosp. hirees
34 Turn off
35 Fictional crime family
36 "No lie!"
37 Court VIPs

38 Prohibited
44 Oater prop
45 Elite, in a way
46 "Reservoir Dogs" actor Michael
48 Starts to receive patrons
50 Skin layer
51 Mid-sized ensemble
52 Detours, e.g.: Abbr.
55 Some VCRs
56 Kind of stew

85

BY LEE GLICKSTEIN AND
NANCY SALOMON

ACROSS
1 Math subject
5 Buck
9 Opt to play for pay
14 Et ___
15 "You ___?"
16 Pulitzer-winning biographer Nevins
17 Made dilettantes bitter?
20 Basin Street setting, with "the"
21 Dormer?
22 Verbal deftness
23 Nimitz's title: Abbr.
25 Time to give up
26 Back biters
29 "Cheers" waitress
31 Gem for a Libra, maybe
32 In unison
33 Letter before omega
36 Pushed enlisted men to the breaking point?
40 Dallas-to-Houston dir.
41 Met offerings
42 Half-moon shape
43 Kind of committee
44 Civil
46 Page with views
49 Former Wall St. group
50 Old platters
51 Commando

53 Embarrassing shade
57 Fought to get more money?
60 Eero Saarinen's father
61 Tax-sheltered accts.
62 Surf phenomenon
63 Crucifixes
64 Part of a pool
65 Flabbergast

DOWN
1 Prep for a marathon, with "up"
2 Jai ___
3 "Ally McBeal" lawyer
4 Breeze
5 Reaches the top
6 Disney dog
7 Collected quotes
8 Leo is its logo
9 Spanish feline
10 Bullfight cheer
11 Feather
12 ___ to go
13 Get-go
18 Hidey-hole
19 "American Gigolo" designer
23 Sponsor's purchase
24 Pricey gowns
26 Uncontrollable masses
27 Numbered work
28 Ruff stuff
30 Yucca Flats locale: Abbr.
32 "Ciao"

33 Spitting sound, in comics
34 Thrilled
35 "The light dawns"
37 Sonny
38 '60s German chancellor
39 Standout athletes
43 Confused, and this puzzle's title
44 Tickle pink
45 Letters over a zero

46 Alphabetize
47 São ___
48 Kids' song refrain
52 Skinny dippers?
53 Muffin ingredient
54 Barrel of laughs
55 Son of Rebekah
56 Laura of "Jurassic Park"
58 Trifling amount
59 Lode load

86

BY MICHAEL VUOLO

ACROSS

1 Certificate
6 Scandinavian native
10 Sepulcher
14 Place for a record, briefly
15 Foreign minister under Meir
16 Prefix with -logue
17 Noted fabulist
18 Ruthless
20 Travel aimlessly
22 Article for Mozart
23 Operated
24 Environmentalist's slogan
30 Mohawk River city
32 Piccadilly Circus statue
33 Discount letters
34 Poise
35 Detroit dud
37 "A ___ ...": kids' song beginning
38 Lodge frequenter
39 Maned antelopes
40 Blues guitarist John
41 Search all over
45 According to
46 Measure up
47 Make a difference, so to speak

54 Italy's largest body of water
55 Naturalist John et al.
57 Writer Haley
58 Expresses disdain
59 Book with legends
60 Saucy
61 Ballesteros on the links
62 Sprig in a bouquet garni

DOWN

1 Place to unwind
2 Order at the dinner table?
3 Santa ___
4 How Shepard's "Cowboys" is performed, e.g.
5 Whitney Houston, for one
6 It's not for everyone
7 Touch
8 Calculating course
9 Lyon-based organization
10 Albania's capital
11 Smell
12 Essence
13 Inclusive choice
19 Gets better
21 Benz ending
24 Pervert, in slang
25 "Siddhartha" author
26 Poetic preposition
27 Suitable place?

28 German earth
29 Rare trick taker
30 Pac-12 team
31 Tailor's chalk ingredient
35 Beseeches
36 "I should have known that!"
37 Six-time A.L. RBI leader
39 Shorthand inventor
40 Old developer
42 On deck

43 Musical with the song "Summer Nights"
44 Order foundation
47 Put one's hands together
48 Hearty partner
49 Oslo's river
50 Faithful
51 Home theater purchase
52 Bell-shaped flower
53 Small amount
56 Fresno-to-L.A. direction

87

BY ALAN ARBESFELD

ACROSS
1 Wouk captain
6 Migrating fish
10 Bellyache
14 Extreme
15 Mood
16 "A Treatise of Human Nature" author
17 Bury
18 Peak no.
19 Samoa's capital
20 Menlo Park monogram
21 One telling the naked truth?
24 Mountain lake
25 Gossip's tidbit, with "the"
26 Taxi stand?
31 French wine valley
32 Returned
37 Lodges
38 Golfer's concern
40 Jai ___
41 Base
43 Sean of "Bulworth"
44 Animal farm activity?
47 Request
51 Prefix with polis
52 Hypnotist?
55 Ring org.
58 Booze it up
59 Skin cream ingredient
60 Sounded satisfied
62 One-sided victory
63 Amoeba habitat
64 One of Chekhov's "Three Sisters"
65 Gets off the fence
66 "Show Me the Way" rock group
67 Bewildered

DOWN
1 Leave
2 Radius neighbor
3 Kitchen finish
4 Prior to
5 It's picked up regularly
6 Caterer's supply
7 Green target
8 One more time
9 Marine
10 Monastery emanation
11 Pakistani coin
12 Wrong
13 Hardly Mr. Nice Guy
22 JFK datum
23 Assignment
24 Like aphorisms
26 Go ape, with "out"
27 Unmatched
28 Brie feature
29 Handy
30 Tours turndown
33 Low range
34 Prefix with graph
35 Nod dweller
36 Checkers goal

178

38 Astronomers' references
39 Kids' card game
42 Clog, say
43 Reason for a siren
45 Sexy
46 Pro
47 National Leaguer until 2012
48 Deign
49 Shot

50 Guides under the strings
53 Tons
54 Sharp competitor
55 Pro
56 1885 Motorwagen maker
57 "___ in the Life": Beatles song
61 Uris hero

88

BY PAULA GAMACHE

ACROSS
1 "Clueless" catchphrase
5 Historic gold rush town
9 Please, in Potsdam
14 Glassmaker Lalique
15 Word to one who isn't listening
16 Company in 2002 news
17 First name in old talk shows
18 Napa growth
19 Elementary particles
20 Advice from Andy Rooney, part 1
23 Incarnation of Vishnu
24 "Dies ___"
25 Advice, part 2
30 Sway
31 Diamond figures
32 Hiss relative
34 Botch
35 Greek consonants
36 Lampblack source
37 Boxer from Cal., e.g.
38 17th-century actress Gwyn
40 Old Testament book with 150 entries
42 Advice, part 3
45 Hold, in a diner
46 New York county bordering Ontario

47 End of advice
52 Composer Massenet
53 One of Chekhov's "Three Sisters"
54 An essay may be part of it
56 Circle lines
57 Holiday number
58 Move, in real estate jargon
59 Rob Roy et al.
60 Some nobility
61 Outer: Prefix

DOWN
1 Shirt part
2 Go after
3 Memo words
4 Aptly named medicinal plant
5 Sailor, perhaps
6 Canton resident
7 Captain's offering
8 Retired, as a professor
9 Laments
10 Hardened
11 Put one's foot down
12 Loads
13 Nav. rank
21 Chopped hors d'oeuvre
22 Small songbird
25 Income source
26 University of Maine city
27 With indifference

28 Deadly virus
29 Not tight
30 "60 Minutes" network
33 NFL tiebreakers
35 Company subdivisions
36 "I agree"
38 Moby Dick, to Ahab
39 Splice, e.g.
40 Imposing entryways
41 Quarter-deck?
43 "Get going!"

44 First speed-of-sound breaker
47 Investigative govt. gp. created in 1938
48 Ray of "Battle Cry"
49 Weena's people, in a Wells novel
50 Corp. leader
51 Fountain order
52 Some coll. students
55 Low in a lea

1

F	A	D	S		L	A	M	E		G	A	P	E	S
A	B	E	L		A	L	A	S		A	D	O	P	T
Q	U	E	U	E	T	I	P	S		Z	O	W	I	E
S	T	R	I	V	E		L	A	G	E	R			
			C	O	X		E	Y	E	B	E	A	M	S
L	A	P	E	L				N	O	R	M	A	L	
E	P	A		V	E	N	T	E	D		S	U	R	E
T	I	L		E	X	F	I	L	E	S		L	I	E
S	E	A	R		C	L	A	I	R	E		E	N	T
A	C	C	U	S	E		E	S	T	E	S			
T	E	E	B	I	L	L	S		T	N	T			
			A	E	S	O	P		A	T	O	N	C	E
A	C	I	D	S		B	E	E	M	O	V	I	E	S
D	O	N	U	T		E	L	S	E		E	N	O	S
A	Q	A	B	A		S	L	E	D		S	O	S	O

2

C	H	O	C		H	A	U	L		E	G	A	D	S
L	E	N	O		S	O	S	O		A	E	S	O	P
E	L	E	M		T	R	U	C	E	S	T	O	R	Y
A	L	I	B	I		T	A	I	N	T	S			
N	U	D	E	D	E	A	L		C	L	E	V	E	R
E	V	A	D	E	R			H	E	A	V	E	H	O
D	A	S		A	N	D	I	E		E	L	S	E	
			B	L	O	O	M	M	O	O	N			
S	E	A	L		Z	A	P	P	A		A	G	R	
S	C	R	A	P	P	Y		E	T	O	I	L	E	
R	O	S	C	O	E		D	U	D	E	D	R	O	P
			K	E	R	N	E	L		S	E	R	B	O
T	O	O	T	T	I	M	I	N	G		S	A	U	R
S	T	A	I	R		E	S	A	I		S	I	L	T
P	O	K	E	Y		X	M	E	N		A	D	E	S

3

A	S	A	P		P	A	R	E		L	A	U	D	S
S	U	B	S		O	M	E	N		E	C	L	A	T
T	R	E	E		L	I	D	O		S	T	A	L	E
I	F	L	U	N	K	E	D	L	A	T	I	N	I	N
			D	O	A		A	P	E					
M	O	T	O	R	I	N	G		T	R	I	P	O	D
A	R	I		S	N	O	R	E		C	A	C	O	
C	O	L	L	E	G	E	I	T	H	O	U	G	H	T
O	N	E	S		L	E	T	I	T		E	R	E	
N	O	S	T	E	R		F	E	A	T	U	R	E	S
			R	U	T		W	O	N					
C	A	E	S	A	R	W	A	S	A	S	A	L	A	D
P	U	T	T	S		I	S	I	T		B	E	D	E
A	N	N	I	E		L	E	A	H		L	A	Z	E
S	T	A	R	R		L	A	M	A		E	D	E	R

4

P	I	Q	U	E		N	A	C	L		M	A	Z	E
E	R	U	P	T		E	T	U	I		O	M	E	N
W	A	I	S	T		S	E	R	F	B	O	A	R	D
			C	A	S	T		L	E	A	N	T	O	S
A	T	T	A		H	E	S		T	I	L			
M	A	I	L	C	H	A	U	V	I	N	I	S	T	
A	R	M	E	D		R	I	M		T	H	U	G	
N	I	B		S	H	A	R	P	E	R		O	R	R
A	F	R	O		I	L	E		B	O	O	N	E	
F	E	U	D	A	L	A	C	T	I	V	I	T	Y	
			T	O	W		L	O	W		E	N	O	S
S	O	N	A	T	A	S		M	O	O	R			
K	N	I	G	H	T	C	A	P		F	J	O	R	D
E	T	T	E		H	A	I	L		F	O	L	I	O
W	O	E	S		A	N	D	Y		S	Y	D	O	W

5

A	S	S	T		R	I	D	E	S		R	O	T	E
L	E	A	H		A	B	O	V	E		A	B	B	R
P	A	G	E	W	I	N	N	E	R		M	O	A	N
S	T	A	T	E	N		G	R	I	P	P	E	R	S
			A	B	B	A		T	A	L	C			
U	P	S		O	R	E		T	A	R	T	A	R	
S	E	A	P	O	W	E	R		E	N	I	S	L	E
H	A	T	E	R		A	N	T		E	M	A	I	L
E	L	A	N	D	S		S	A	U	T	E	R	N	E
R	E	N	N	E	T		T	I	S		S	E	T	
			F	R	E	D		L	E	N	S			
A	T	T	E	S	T	E	D		L	O	W	B	O	Y
S	H	I	V		S	E	R	G	E	B	I	L	K	O
P	A	N	E		O	R	E	O	S		F	U	R	L
S	T	A	R		N	E	W	T	S		T	E	A	K

6

S	C	A	R	P		S	A	H	L		O	P	E	N
H	A	L	E	R		A	L	E	E		B	I	D	E
A	M	I	L	E		H	E	R	A		L	E	D	A
L	E	V	E	E	T	A	X	E	S		O	R	A	L
E	L	E	A	N	O	R			H	A	N	G		
			S	E	S	A	M	E		E	G	R	E	T
E	L	D	E	R	S		A	N	D	S		O	D	E
M	O	O	D		E	M	O	T	E		S	U	I	T
M	A	C		T	S	A	R		A	D	E	P	T	S
A	N	K	L	E		S	I	E	R	R	A			
			R	O	M	E		S	T	O	P	G	A	P
S	L	O	W		B	E	R	T	H	P	L	A	C	E
C	O	O	K		O	N	E	A		S	A	B	R	A
A	C	M	E		N	Y	E	T		I	N	L	E	T
R	O	S	Y		Y	A	L	E		N	E	E	D	Y

7

H	E	R	A		S	A	C	R	A		B	A	S	H
O	X	E	N		U	N	L	E	D		A	B	E	E
M	U	S	I	C	S	C	A	L	E		T	S	A	R
A	D	O	L	P	H		Y	I	N		H	E	W	
G	E	L		R	I	D		V	I	N	T	N	E	R
E	D	E	R		B	O	N	E		O	U	T	E	R
			A	D	A	M	A		I	M	B	E	D	S
		M	I	R	R	O	R	I	M	A	G	E		
A	L	I	N	E	S		C	A	P	R	I			
M	A	S	S	A		G	O	G	O		N	A	I	R
B	U	S	H	M	A	N		O	R	R		D	D	E
	G	P	O		R	A	M		T	O	P	D	O	G
W	H	E	W		G	R	E	A	T	B	A	S	I	N
E	I	N	E		U	L	T	R	A		C	O	D	A
E	N	T	R		E	S	S	E	X		E	N	O	L

8

O	M	A	H	A		J	I	B	E		O	W	L	S
N	E	G	E	V		A	R	E	A		R	H	E	A
C	A	R	R	I	E	C	A	T	T		F	I	A	T
U	T	E		A	T	O	N		T	E	R	P		
E	Y	E		T	O	B	I	A	S	W	O	L	F	F
			L	E	N	S		T	O	I		A	R	E
I	R	E		C	O	S	T		W	O	N			
A	M	O	S	A	L	O	N	Z	O	S	T	A	G	G
T	I	S		T	O	R	N		A	Y	S			
I	T	S		E	R	A		G	M	E	N			
C	A	P	T	A	I	N	K	I	D	D		I	S	H
	T	E	R	M		A	M	I	S		L	I	E	
A	I	R	Y		J	I	M	M	I	E	F	O	X	X
L	O	O	M		A	D	E	E		L	E	V	E	E
A	N	T	E		B	A	N	S		S	N	E	R	D

9

D	E	B	T	S		R	O	T	C		S	O	F	T
A	R	R	A	U		A	F	A	R		L	A	L	A
T	R	I	P	C	O	F	F	E	E	M	A	K	E	R
E	S	C		H	U	T	S		S	U	N	S	E	T
			K	V	A	S	S		P	S	S	T		
A	T	L	A	S	T		B	R	I	T		W	H	O
P	E	A	L			S	L	I	D	E	S	H	O	W
T	R	Y	V	O	D	K	A	M	A	R	T	I	N	I
T	R	E	E	H	O	U	S	E			A	T	E	N
O	A	R		W	E	N	T		R	A	T	E	D	G
			D	E	S	K		R	E	N	E	W		
O	C	C	U	L	T		M	E	A	N		A	L	B
T	R	I	L	L	I	N	S	T	R	U	C	T	O	R
I	O	T	A		M	A	G	I		A	R	E	N	A
S	P	E	C		E	Y	R	E		L	Y	R	I	C

10

L	A	B	S		M	O	R	A	N		M	A	S	S
I	N	R	E		E	R	A	T	O		U	S	E	R
E	G	A	D		A	S	N	E	R		N	O	T	I
D	E	C	A	R	L	O	G	A	M	B	I	N	O	
E	L	E	N	I			M	A	O			E	F	T
R	O	D		C	A	L	L		A	I	M	T	O	
			U	K	R	A	I	N	E		M	A	W	R
	O	B	R	I	A	N	B	O	I	T	A	N	O	
S	N	U	G		M	E	R	I	N	O	S			
A	C	R	E	S			A	R	E	A		M	A	E
L	E	N		O	L	E			S	C	A	D	S	
	M	A	C	D	O	N	A	L	D	T	R	U	M	P
H	O	B	O		B	A	S	I	E		E	M	I	R
A	R	L	O		O	C	E	A	N		S	A	R	I
H	E	E	L		S	T	A	R	T		S	U	E	T

11

A	D	I	M		C	A	T	S		A	F	O	A	M
N	O	N	O		A	G	H	A		G	U	M	M	O
T	H	E	H	U	N	T	E	R		O	R	I	O	N
			V	E	G		I	D	O	U	B	T	I	T
	H	I	G	H	S	O	C	I	E	T	Y			
S	O	D	A		A	N	E		D	I	S	B	A	R
T	M	E	N		R	E	M				A	R	I	
P	I	N	S		G	I	A	N	T		M	R	E	D
	A	E	C			N	A	G		O	R	N	E	
T	R	E	A	T	Y		C	I	I		T	E	A	R
			S	H	I	P	O	F	F	O	O	L	S	
P	L	A	T	I	N	U	M		O	R	R			
O	A	T	E	R		N	E	I	G	H	B	O	R	S
S	N	O	R	T		I	T	S	A		U	L	E	E
H	E	N	N	Y		C	H	O	P		S	L	A	T

12

P	I	S	A		H	A	Y		F	A	I	R		
A	N	E	W		U	E	L	E		L	I	N	E	
S	W	E	E	T	N	L	O	W	D	A	D	D	Y	
S	I	N		Y	I	P	E		E	S	A	U		
A	T	T	A	R	S		N	E	H		C	A	T	
T	H	O	R		O	L	E	O	S	C	O	T	C	H
			C	A	N	O	E	S		A	R	E	N	A
H	A	S	T	A		A	R	T		R	I	D	E	R
A	S	T	I	R		T	I	R	A	D	E			
Z	I	R	C	O	N	H	E	A	D		N	O	P	E
E	N	E		N	E	E		R	E	T	A	I	L	
	U	S	S	R		F	A	I	L		R	E	A	
A	S	T	R	O	T	U	R	F	S	K	I	R	T	
R	E	L	O		O	M	I	T		E	N	C	E	
P	L	O	D		W	E	D		A	G	E	D		

13

A	B	E	E		R	A	S	P		B	E	G	A	N
T	E	N	N		O	S	L	O		E	V	O	K	E
L	A	Z	E		T	T	O	P		B	E	H	A	D
A	N	Y	R	E	C	I	P	E	F	O	R	A		
S	I	M	O	N			Y	A	P		L	V	I	
T	E	E		T	H	A	M	E	S		A	V	E	C
			D	I	A	N	E			C	L	E	R	K
S	P	E	E	C	H	S	H	O	U	L	D	S	A	Y
M	A	Y	B	E			T	A	L	I	A			
O	P	E	S		I	N	A	S	E	C		S	T	A
G	A	P		I	T	O			H	O	P	I	N	
			A	D	D	S	H	O	R	T	E	N	I	N	G
U	N	T	I	E		O	R	E	O		I	N	G	E
M	E	C	C	A		P	E	N	N		C	A	L	L
A	C	H	E	S		E	S	T	E		E	L	E	A

14

Q	T	I	P		J	A	V	E	R	T		O	R	A
U	R	N	S		U	N	I	A	T	E		P	U	T
O	U	R	S	O	N	N	E	V	E	R		I	S	T
D	E	E		D	E	E	R	E		R	I	A	T	A
			T	I	A				T	A	C	T	I	C
P	I	C	K	S	U	P	T	H	E	C	H	E	C	K
E	L	I	O	T		E	R	A	S	E				
W	E	D		D	R	O	S	S			A	L	B	
			B	U	I	L	T		R	O	D	E	O	
Y	O	U	R	E	A	L	L	Y	H	A	V	E	T	O
E	N	R	O	L	L			U	N	O				
L	A	B	E	L		A	E	T	N	A		S	P	A
P	G	A		H	A	N	D	I	T	T	O	H	I	M
E	E	N		O	N	D	I	N	E		P	O	N	E
D	R	E		P	E	S	T	E	R		T	E	E	N

15

T	O	T	A	L		V	S	O	P		D	A	N	E
A	M	U	S	E		L	O	N	E		E	L	A	L
R	O	B	I	N	B	A	N	K	S		S	A	R	I
P	O	E	S	I	E	S		P	O	R	T	I	C	O
			E	N	I	D			E	R	N	S	T	
R	O	L	A	N	D	C	O	F	F	E	Y			
E	X	A	L	T			G	O	L	F		C	O	W
B	E	S	T		C	A	R	E	Y		E	R	G	O
A	N	T		L	A	N	A			A	M	O	R	E
			H	O	R	A	C	E	S	C	O	P	E	S
A	D	D	O	N			E	X	E	C				
T	O	U	R	I	S	M		E	R	O	T	I	C	A
E	L	A	N		W	A	L	T	E	R	W	A	L	L
A	C	N	E		I	D	E	E		D	I	G	U	P
M	E	E	T		G	E	A	R		S	N	O	B	S

16

S	A	S	S		A	M	A	T		A	R	E	A	S
A	L	A	I		L	A	C	E		Z	E	R	O	S
K	I	N	G	O	F	T	H	E	J	U	G	G	L	E
S	T	E	N	O			T	E	N	U	R	E		
			P	O	S	E		A	G	E	N	D	A	S
A	T	N	O		A	L	E	G			T	U	B	E
T	R	A	S	H	Y		N	E	V	A		B	B	C
B	O	S	T	O	N	S	T	R	A	G	G	L	E	R
E	I	S		G	O	E	R		L	O	U	I	S	E
S	K	E	W		T	Y	P	E		I	N	S	T	
T	A	R	I	F	F	S		E	T	O	N			
			D	I	E	S	E	L		S	N	A	R	E
J	I	G	G	L	E	A	L	L	T	H	E	W	A	Y
O	C	T	E	T		I	S	E	E		S	O	R	E
T	E	E	T	H		L	A	T	E		S	L	E	D

17

```
A M F M . R O L E X . W U S S
L E I A . I R A N I . A N N A
G I R L . B E T T I N G Z O O
A R E A . B O E R . O N I O N
. D R N O . S T E P P E
B A R K I N G M E T E R
A L I E N . H A V E S . B O B
R E L Y . M E R I T . D O N E
B E L . Q A N D A . P O N C E
. B U T T I N G G R E E N
A F L O A T . L A I C
B L I P S . A S T A . S H A M
B E E P I N G T O M . D I V A
E S T E . B R A V O . A N O N
S H O D . C A G E R . Y A W N
```

18

```
A P E S . B A M B I . S L O P
B E L L . B R A I N . H A V E
E S A U . G E N T S . A M E N
L O N G J U A N S I L V E R
. F A N S . S E E
S A F E R . C I T A D E L S
U R L S . D R O V E R . N E T
M E E T G I O V A N N I D O E
U N E . O R I E N T . D E N T
P A T E N T L Y . A I D E S
. R E Y . A S T O
D E A R J E A N L E T T E R
P E A S . O M N I A . B O D E
E L S E . K I T T Y . O M E N
P I E R . E L I A S . X E N O
```

19

```
D E C A F . A L B S . E V A S
I R A N I . L I E U . N A R C
V I L E F O L D E R . C U B A
. M E T . O F F C O L O R
C A V O R T S . S A R T R E
B E A N S . H O V . R E F
E S S E . W I S E T O . I S H
R O T . V A N C L U B . N N E
S P F . I N T A C T . A D A R
. O N T . O R R . A C E R B
U P R O A R . O R D E R L Y
N E W B L O O D . E O S
B A A L . V O C A L P O I N T
A C R E . E N O S . T U R F S
R E D S . R A N K . S T A L K
```

20

```
F E L I Z . B E T S . D O F F
I R A T E . U P O N . A L A I
G I V E N . L E S E . T I R E
. C A M I L L E C A R A V A N
. S T E M . A K A . E D D
B A R . H O O F . S N O
A R I A . N O L I . C L O N E
J A C Q U E S I N T H E B O X
A B O U T . E N N A . S E M I
. A H A . T O K E . Y E T
U M P . E L S . C E N T
P I E R R E P R E S S U R E
T A R A . R E I N . U B O L T
O M I T . T A L C . R A D I O
N I L E . S K E E . E S S A Y
```

21

```
S A T I S F Y . E C L O G U E
S P A C E R S . S L I P O N S
N O M I N E E . C O V E R U P
. P E T E R P A N E N E M Y
. S A W . O R E
L A I T . H O O P . B M O C S
E D D . S E A R . B A A B A A
T H E A T E R D E L I V E R Y
G O S P E L . E C O N . Y E A
O C T E T . A V O W . E S T H
. M L I . P A X
B A S E B A L L P I T C H
A U P A I R S . A P R I O R I
T R U S T E E . P E A S A N T
T A R T E S T . A S P E R S E
```

22

```
A S H E . J E T S . L O S E
L I A R . I D E A L . A X L E
I N S O . B U R M A . Z E A L
C A T T L E C R O S S I N G
E I E I O . E A T I N
. C O M B . L E A D S
C A B . M E A N S G O S L O W
A C E S . A N I T A . S E M I
T H A T O L D B U L L . S E M
S E N O R . B E E S
. P E A R S . S U P E R
I S S O M E C O W S B E A U
A N T I . S H A V E . L E V I
S T A G . T A L E S . E V E N
H O R N . B E N T . T E S S
```

23

```
P S A T . S T I R . A W A I T
M A N Y . H E B E . B A S S O
S N I C K E R E D . A P I N G
. A M O O S E G O E S I N T O
R N A . D A S . G E T
E T T A . A B A R . I M E T
D O E R S . L I E N . A V E
A N D T H E B A R T E N D E R
N I L . A R U N . T O E R R
T O Y S . A S K S . G A G A
. I T S . U A E . S R S
W H Y T H E L O N G F A C E
H O U S E . I N B E T W E E N
O R R I S . O D O R . A N N A
M A I N E . N E W S . R E S T
```

24

```
M A T T H A U . A D E P T S
A M O R O U S . M O S A I C S
T A K I N G A B A C K S E A T
S H E A . E G O . S I E R R A
. S C R E A M . M O S E Y
L A S S O S . E R O S
A N T I C . K A L E . R I O
K N O C K I N G O F F W O R K
E A P . K E E N . L A B O R
. P L E A . H E L E N A
G A B L E . D E N I E R
U N R E S T . G I G . U C L A
S T E A L I N G T H E S H O W
T E N S I L E . R E W E A V E
S T E E L E . O R E S T E S
```

25

R	S	V	P		W	O	O	D	S		S	M	O	G
U	T	I	L		I	N	L	E	T		P	I	P	E
M	A	T	A		P	L	E	B	E		O	M	E	N
B	R	A	I	S	E	Y	O	U	R	V	O	I	C	E
A	R	E	N	T			S	N	E	A	K			
			J	U	D	O		K	O	P		M	O	M
A	B	B	A		A	W	L		O	S	A	K	A	
B	L	E	N	D	M	E	Y	O	U	R	E	A	R	S
C	A	T	E	R		E	O	N		X	M	A	S	
S	H	E		U	A	R		H	I	C	K			
			V	I	T	A	L		R	I	N	S	E	
B	R	E	A	D	T	H	E	R	I	O	T	A	C	T
A	H	E	M		E	R	M	A	S		T	O	A	T
H	E	L	P		S	A	U	C	E		E	M	M	A
S	A	S	S		T	H	R	E	E		N	I	P	S

26

M	A	I	N	M	A	N		S	T	O	P	G	A	P
I	U	S	E	D	T	O		A	I	R	R	A	G	E
S	T	U	D	I	E	S		S	N	O	O	Z	E	S
S	O	P			H	A	S	H		B	E	N	T	
			S	C	O	O	T		A	L	E	R	T	S
B	E	S	N	O	W	W	H	I	T	E				
O	T	T	E	R	S		L	A	S	T	G	A	S	P
O	N	E	A	D		B	E	N		S	U	P	E	R
B	A	N	K	O	N	I	T		A	L	L	P	R	O
				B	U	T	I	D	R	I	F	T	E	D
T	O	M	C	A	T		C	O	M	P	S			
O	D	O	R		C	A	S	T			U	F	O	
P	O	T	O	M	A	C		I	C	E	D	T	E	A
O	U	T	P	O	S	T		M	A	E	W	E	S	T
G	L	O	S	S	E	S		E	N	L	I	S	T	S

27

W	A	S	T	E		M	A	I	M		Z	O	N	E
R	I	P	E	N		A	U	D	I		O	V	E	R
E	R	R	E	D		G	R	O	G		D	A	L	I
S	E	E	N		G	N	A	S	H	V	I	L	L	E
T	R	E	A	C	L	E			T	E	A			
			G	N	A	T	K	I	N	G	C	O	L	E
A	T	T	E	N	D		I	O	T	A		M	I	X
G	O	A	D		B	T	U		M	A	M	E		
O	R	B		T	H	E	E		T	I	A	R	A	S
G	N	U	F	O	U	N	D	L	A	N	D			
			O	S	S		A	N	N	E	T	T	E	
G	N	E	I	S	S	W	O	R	K		L	E	A	D
R	I	A	L		A	R	I	D		M	I	A	M	I
A	C	R	E		R	I	S	E		O	N	S	E	T
B	E	N	D		S	T	E	R		B	E	E	R	S

28

D	E	B	S		S	T	A	T		F	O	C	U	S
I	G	E	T		A	I	R	E		S	N	A	F	U
A	R	G	O		I	N	C	H		H	E	R	O	N
L	E	G	G	E	D	T	H	E	W	A	Y			
S	T	A	I	N	S		E	R	R	A	N	D	S	
			R	E	D	O	A	K		U	P	R	O	O	T
B	A	S	S	O		L	A	W	N		D	R	N	O
A	C	T		N	E	S	T	E	G	G		M	O	W
C	H	O	P		T	O	I	L		E	L	A	T	E
H	O	O	R	A	H		E	L	I	N	O	R		
S	O	L	O	M	O	N		N	I	N	E	P	M	
			C	E	S	T	L	A	V	E	G	G	I	E
N	O	F	U	N		E	A	S	E		A	G	E	D
A	W	A	R	D		S	K	I	N		R	A	T	A
H	E	X	E	S		T	E	N	T		M	E	A	L

29

S	I	M	I		A	L	M	A		A	M	O	R	E
I	R	I	S	H	N	A	M	E	P	R	E	F	I	X
C	O	M	M	O	N	B	L	O	O	D	T	Y	P	E
K	N	I	S	H		E	I	N	E		R	O	E	S
			O	I	L			H	O	U	R			
	N	O	A	H	S		M	O	P	E				
S	Y	M	B	O	L	F	O	R	O	X	Y	G	E	N
B	R	A	E		A	U	R	A	L		A	E	R	O
W	O	R	D	I	N	M	A	N	Y	H	Y	M	N	S
				A	D	E	N		P	O	S	S	E	
			A	D	A	M		L	S	D				
K	C	A	L		M	A	Y	O		M	A	R	D	I
O	H	M	A	B	B	R	E	V	I	A	T	I	O	N
C	O	N	T	R	A	C	T	I	O	N	O	F	O	F
H	O	S	E	A		S	I	N	N		Z	E	R	O

30

A	L	E	A	F		I	T	E	M		S	H	A	H
L	A	R	G	O		G	E	N	A		E	E	R	O
F	I	R	E	C	O	U	N	T	R	Y	H	A	I	R
			R	U	N	A	T		T	E	R	R	A	S
S	N	O		S	Y	N		W	I	M		N	N	E
W	O	R	D	E	X	A	M	I	N	E	R	O	A	D
A	W	A	R	D		A	L	I	N	E				
N	I	L	E		B	O	N	D	S		T	R	A	M
			D	I	E	T	S		A	R	E	N	A	
W	I	N	D	S	T	R	E	E	T	B	O	N	E	S
I	C	U		L	A	O		L	O	S		O	T	T
G	E	T	S	E	T		A	N	T	I	S			
W	A	L	K	S	E	C	T	I	O	N	T	O	W	N
A	G	E	E		S	O	O	N		T	A	L	I	A
M	E	T	E		T	Y	P	O		H	Y	A	T	T

31

S	L	A	T		C	R	A	S	S		H	A	I	L
H	I	G	H		H	E	L	O	T		O	U	R	S
A	T	R	I		O	B	E	S	E		S	T	A	T
W	H	E	N	Y	O	U	C	O	M	E	T	O		
M	E	E	K	E	S	T			R	E	M	A	N	
			O	N	E		B	R	A	S	S	A	G	E
D	R	A	F	T		Y	E	A	R		S	T	O	W
R	E	D		A	F	O	R	K	I	N		I	R	E
A	G	U	A		O	G	R	E		O	S	C	A	R
G	A	L	L	E	R	I	A		A	R	M			
	S	L	A	C	K		A	L	M	O	N	D	S	
		T	H	E	R	O	A	D	T	A	K	E	I	T
F	L	O	E		E	T	U	D	E		I	R	M	A
D	O	R	M		A	R	D	O	R		E	V	E	R
R	O	S	Y		P	A	I	N	S		R	E	S	T

32

G	R	A	M		D	O	D	O		O	N	T	O	P
R	I	C	E		E	R	I	C		M	E	H	T	A
A	S	L	O	N	G	A	S	T	H	E	R	E	I	S
N	E	U	W	I	R	T	H		E	L	D	E	S	T
			G	E	O		P	I	E	S				
A	N	O	T	H	E	R	T	E	S	T		M	R	S
R	I	G	H	T		H	O	T	S	H	E	E	T	
T	E	R	I		C	O	R	N	S		O	R	S	O
S	C	E	N	E	O	N	E		S	O	C	I	O	
Y	E	S		Y	O	U	W	I	L	L	F	I	N	D
			R	E	P	S		T	A	U				
S	I	M	I	L	E		S	A	N	S	K	R	I	T
P	R	A	Y	E	R	I	N	S	C	H	O	O	L	S
E	A	T	A	T		D	I	C	E		L	I	S	P
D	E	A	L	S		S	P	A	T		A	L	A	S

33

```
T O N G S   M A G I     S O N S
A B O I L   I R A Q   A V O W
B I L L Y C L U B S   L A V A
S E A L   L A M E   M U L A N
  S N I P E     S L O T
    A L O O F   O N E A L S
H E N N A   M R G O O D B A R
U Z I   T H E E A S T   L I T
H I P J O I N T S   O P E R A
S O S O O N   S H A N E
    U N D O     B E A T S
D I O R S   N O M E   R E N E
I C O N   B E A U T Y S P O T
V E N A   A U K S   M O I R A
E T A L   A P S E   A N D E S
```

34

```
W H Y D O N T   S M A S H U P
Y E S O R N O   T I N W A R E
E M E N D E D   U N H I N G E
S P R E E     E N G E N D E R
      A P S E   L U G
W E C A L L E L V E S     C A M
I M U P   E A S E   E L O P E
L I B E R A L   L Y R I C A L
C R E D O   A R C O   M O R E
O S S   S U B O R D I N A T E
    S A T   L O A M
R E P A R T E E     P L A N S
I R O N I E S   C L A U D I A
D I E T E R S   B I L L E T S
E N M A S S E   C L A U S E S
```

35

```
D O E R   I N N   S T O L E S
A L L I   R O I   C H A I S E
K I N G K O N G   H E T M A N
O V I   I N C H   S H O U T
T E N A M   E T U D E S
A T O P   A T R A   R H O
    A M T   F A I R D E A L
A F A C E I N T H E C R O W D
A B S E N T E E   S H E
H I P   A L E R   A A R P
    S T E R N O   O D D E R
J U L I A   I S A W   A D E
O R A L L Y   G A S L I G H T
T A L K I E   H G T   D I E T
S L A Y E R   T E A   S O N Y
```

36

```
B U T T     O P U S   M E C H
O P A R T   M O S T   A L E E
E D G A R   A P S O   K I L N
R O S I E T H E R I V E T E R
  A N Y W A Y   C A M E B Y
H E L M   O N E M I L E
A L O A F   T O S S   S A T
D E N N I S T H E M E N A C E
J A G   N U K E   S O M M E
  M I M O S A S   A M E N
A G E I S M   A L B A N Y
T O M T H E P I P E R S S O N
S U I T   D A L I   A W O K E
E R L E   U P O N   M E S A S
A D E N   P A R E   R A Y S
```

37

```
S L E D S   R E V S   H A L O
A U D I O   A R C H   E L A N
C L A S S E S A R E A B O R E
S U M P   U P S   T R E K S
    O U R   T A L E
T H I S F O O D I S A W F U L
R O M E O   L I N K S   E S E
A V A   A D A M S   L A G
M E G   A R E N A   G L O G G
P L E A S E S E N D M O N E Y
    L S A T   E T C
M A P L E   E L F   A S P S
I J U S T G O T A T A T T O O
F A R E   U R N S   V O I L A
F R E T   Y E A H   E R R O R
```

38

```
A W A G   R O T E   J I B E S
R A R E   E X E S   A D A M S
A L M A   V E R A   B O L O S
B L A R N E Y R U B B L E
I O N   I R E   B A S A L T
A P I E C E   F A Q   R A H
    G E N I A L   S P I T E
B L A N D P R A C T I C E
B R I N E   S C R E E N
I A M   W E E   T R A D E D
Z S A Z S A   M A E   A A A
  B L A N K A C C O U N T S
O D E O N   L U G E   H U S H
W Y A T T   E L E A   O B I E
L E N Y A   E D E N   H E N S
```

39

```
G A S     G R A T E   T A C T
R A T S   L A T E X   A V O W
A R I A   E N E R O   C O M O
C O F F E E I S N T   O N E S
I N F E R     S I S   L O T
E S S   A M F M   C A B A N A
    I S A A C S   N A D I R
  S A M U E L G O L D W Y N
U L N A R   L E N T I L
M A I M E D   E S S E   M P S
P M S   S U M   G O O U T
I D E S   M Y C U P O F T E A
R U T H   D R O N E   M E R V
E N T O   U N L I T   E T T E
S K E W   M A T T E   S O S
```

40

```
F R O M   S A G A S   I S M S
A E R O   A D U L T   S O A K
T M E N   G A L L O   L U C Y
C O L D C O M F O R T E R
A T S E A     T E A   M A T
T E E   C H E M   D O C I L E
    S T E R E O     A L E X
D R A W I N G A B L A N K E T
A U R A   O N I O N S
D E E P L Y   S T U N   I N D
A R A   E V A   A S F O R
  C O V E R L E T S T O R Y
S H O W   T R O V E   A N T I
A I D E   T O N E S   B L O C
W E E D   E W E R S   S Y N E
```

41

W	H	Y	I	S	T	H	E	■	T	I	M	E	O	F
H	E	A	R	T	I	E	R	■	A	N	E	M	I	A
A	L	L	E	Y	C	A	T	■	U	S	A	B	L	Y
T	O	T	■	E	S	T	E	S	■	■	D	R	Y	S
S	T	A	B	■	■	E	S	E	■	M	O	O	■	■
■	■	A	J	A	R	■	D	A	Y	W	I	T	H	■
S	E	A	G	O	D	■	E	G	I	S	■	D	U	O
E	M	U	■	S	L	O	W	E	S	T	■	E	N	D
N	I	N	■	E	A	S	E	■	L	I	B	R	A	S
T	R	A	F	F	I	C	■	D	E	C	O	■	■	■
■	■	T	I	S	■	A	C	E	■	■	P	C	B	S
E	T	U	N	■	R	E	S	I	T	■	A	A	H	■
P	A	R	I	A	H	■	S	I	D	E	L	I	N	E
I	D	E	A	T	E	■	A	L	A	C	A	R	T	E
C	A	L	L	E	D	■	R	U	S	H	H	O	U	R

42

A	P	T	E	S	T	■	I	T	T	O	■	T	L	C
S	I	E	S	T	A	■	P	H	E	N	■	R	I	O
K	E	P	T	I	N	■	S	O	M	E	T	I	M	E
F	R	E	E	E	N	T	E	R	P	R	I	S	E	■
O	R	E	■	S	A	O	■	P	E	S	E	T	A	S
R	E	S	T	■	■	A	V	E	■	■	A	D	A	■
■	■	■	H	O	R	D	E	■	P	R	A	T	E	D
■	S	E	E	E	Y	E	T	O	E	Y	E	■	■	■
U	G	A	N	D	A	■	R	H	I	N	E	■	■	■
S	U	P	■	■	A	S	I	■	■	S	A	D	A	■
E	M	P	O	W	E	R	■	N	R	A	■	F	I	T
■	T	H	R	E	E	E	G	G	O	M	E	L	E	T
G	R	I	D	I	R	O	N	■	P	I	R	A	T	E
E	E	R	■	G	I	L	A	■	E	D	A	M	E	S
E	E	E	■	H	E	A	T	■	D	E	S	E	R	T

43

L	A	T	S	■	B	L	A	B	■	R	A	B	I	D
O	R	A	L	■	R	E	N	O	■	I	M	E	T	A
O	M	R	I	■	A	V	O	W	■	N	O	T	E	D
K	A	P	P	A	W	E	L	L	■	G	N	A	R	S
U	N	O	P	E	N	E	D	■	N	I	G	H	■	■
P	I	N	E	S	■	■	C	O	N	S	O	L	E	■
■	■	■	R	O	W	B	O	A	T	■	T	O	I	L
J	O	E	■	P	A	R	A	G	O	N	■	K	E	Y
A	R	T	S	■	D	I	R	E	F	U	L	■	■	■
B	R	A	C	K	E	T	■	■	B	I	O	M	E	■
■	■	H	A	I	R	■	P	O	S	I	T	R	O	N
T	R	O	T	S	■	D	E	L	T	A	H	A	N	D
H	U	R	T	S	■	E	D	I	E	■	E	C	R	U
R	E	S	E	E	■	N	A	V	E	■	S	L	O	E
U	S	E	R	S	■	S	L	E	D	■	T	E	E	S

44

S	C	O	U	T	M	O	T	T	O	■	M	O	W	N
I	L	L	N	A	T	U	R	E	D	■	E	P	I	C
L	I	E	I	N	S	T	A	T	E	■	R	A	G	A
K	N	O	X	■	■	S	I	R	S	■	I	L	S	A
Y	E	S	■	B	U	E	N	A	■	A	T	E	■	■
■	■	■	W	A	N	T	■	G	A	S	■	S	E	W
A	S	W	A	R	M	■	P	O	P	S	I	C	L	E
L	O	R	D	B	A	D	E	N	P	O	W	E	L	L
P	H	A	S	E	D	I	N	■	E	R	A	S	E	D
S	O	P	■	R	E	A	■	P	A	T	S	■	■	■
■	■	P	B	S	■	L	A	I	R	S	■	N	R	A
A	R	E	A	■	S	T	A	N	■	■	E	B	A	N
M	U	D	D	■	N	O	N	C	H	A	L	A	N	T
A	B	U	G	■	U	N	D	E	R	S	I	E	G	E
H	Y	P	E	■	B	E	P	R	E	P	A	R	E	D

45

A	L	A	R	M	■	B	L	A	H	■	T	A	R	A
M	A	R	I	A	■	R	O	L	E	■	I	C	O	N
T	H	E	O	N	L	Y	T	I	M	E	T	H	A	T
S	R	A	■	T	O	A	S	T	■	T	H	E	M	E
■	■	■	E	R	I	N	■	■	C	H	E	■	■	■
A	W	O	M	A	N	T	R	U	L	Y	■	A	L	L
G	R	U	B	S	■	■	I	S	O	L	A	B	L	E
G	E	N	E	■	B	U	S	E	D	■	T	E	A	M
I	N	C	R	E	A	S	E	■	■	A	L	A	M	O
E	S	E	■	C	H	A	N	G	E	S	A	M	A	N
■	■	■	N	O	S	■	■	R	A	P	S	■	■	■
B	A	S	E	L	■	W	R	A	T	H	■	M	A	P
I	S	W	H	E	N	H	E	I	S	A	B	A	B	Y
B	E	A	R	■	B	E	A	N	■	L	A	Y	E	R
B	A	B	U	■	A	W	R	Y	■	T	R	A	D	E

46

B	A	C	O	N	■	A	L	I	B	I	■	S	H	E
E	L	O	P	E	■	S	I	R	E	N	■	N	O	R
D	O	P	E	O	P	L	E	I	N	C	H	I	N	A
S	E	E	R	■	Y	E	N	S	■	H	O	P	E	S
■	■	■	A	C	R	E	■	■	S	E	V	E	R	E
U	S	E	T	H	E	P	H	R	A	S	E	■	■	■
R	O	D	E	O	■	■	I	A	N	■	R	A	C	K
G	A	G	■	P	R	E	P	P	E	D	■	B	A	N
E	K	E	S	■	A	L	P	■	■	O	B	E	S	E
■	■	■	N	O	T	F	O	R	A	L	L	T	H	E
A	S	S	U	R	E	■	■	E	T	T	U	■	■	■
S	H	A	F	T	■	P	O	L	O	■	R	E	S	T
C	O	F	F	E	E	I	N	A	M	E	R	I	C	A
I	R	E	■	G	E	T	T	Y	■	R	E	R	A	N
I	T	S	■	A	L	T	O	S	■	E	D	E	N	S

47

P	E	O	N	■	M	I	S	O	■	R	S	V	P	S
E	U	R	O	■	A	N	E	W	■	O	U	I	J	A
E	R	I	N	■	S	C	A	N	■	L	E	A	S	T
L	E	G	O	F	C	A	M	E	L	O	T	■	■	■
S	K	I	■	L	A	M	■	R	O	D	■	N	B	A
■	A	N	G	E	R	E	D	S	P	E	C	I	E	S
■	■	■	A	W	A	R	E	■	E	X	O	C	E	T
W	A	C	S	■	A	N	D	■	■	Z	E	R	O	■
E	L	A	P	S	E	■	S	E	I	Z	E	■	■	■
D	I	R	E	C	T	D	E	S	C	A	N	T	S	■
S	T	D	■	O	R	A	■	T	I	P	■	I	P	O
■	■	■	N	O	E	N	D	I	N	S	I	G	H	T
Q	U	O	I	T	■	D	O	N	E	■	F	R	E	T
B	L	A	K	E	■	E	T	E	S	■	F	I	R	E
S	A	F	E	R	■	R	O	S	S	■	Y	S	E	R

48

P	A	A	R	■	C	P	L	U	S	■	T	W	I	T
O	R	N	E	■	A	R	I	S	E	■	A	E	R	O
N	I	N	A	■	M	A	S	S	E	■	B	A	K	E
Y	O	U	R	R	E	W	A	R	D	F	O	R	■	■
U	S	A	■	E	O	N	■	■	M	O	T	H	S	■
P	O	L	L	S	■	■	T	A	P	S	■	H	A	H
■	■	■	E	T	A	G	E	R	E	■	V	I	N	E
N	O	T	S	T	R	A	N	G	L	I	N	G	■	■
C	O	N	S	■	M	I	M	O	S	A	S	■	■	■
A	G	E	■	G	O	D	S	■	■	N	E	S	T	S
R	O	B	I	N	■	■	Y	A	K	■	T	E	E	■
■	■	Y	O	U	R	T	E	E	N	A	G	E	R	S
E	T	O	N	■	E	W	I	N	G	■	O	R	C	A
V	E	N	I	■	B	A	R	T	S	■	S	E	E	M
E	X	E	C	■	A	S	E	A	T	■	H	O	L	E

49

```
M A L E S | C O A S T | U M P
A M I G O | A F I R E | N O R
D O F O L K S F R O M | B O O
E S T | V E T | P E E N S
| W E A R S | C O L A
D O W N S O U T H S E R V E
D E B I T | R I A | M A I N
U P S | S T E V E N S | B A D
E T T E | A R I | C A L L S
T H E I R B E V E R A G E S
| T R E S | E L A T E
M I R E S | I N T | C O P
A L I | I N D I X I E C U P S
T I C | S A U D I | R A K E S
H A S | T E N O R | S P E N T
```

50

```
G A I N | S I B S | C L A S S
O T R A | E L E A | H O L M S
T H O R | E L A N | I N L A W
M O N K E Y B U S I N E S S
A M O | N A E | N O R T H S
D E N T S | H A R | S A H L
N O T S O H O T | T I O
F U T U R E S M A R K E T
F I N | L A P P E D U P
A L D A | L T S | I S L E S
T E E V E E | I V S | E L K
P R E S E N T C O M P A N Y
L A W N S | A R A T | E P I C
O S A G E | S I R E | L E N A
S T Y E S | A X E D | F R O M
```

51

```
D O N O R | S P A S | M O R E
E L O P E | H A R P | A N O N
B E A T S | A R A L | N E A T
H I T T H E B I G T I M E
V I S C O U S | T R A D E R
E L A I N E | I D E A | A D S
T A R A | S T A N D S
K N O C K E M D E A D
S O L E M N | N E H I
A F T | M O W S | R A G L A N
C L A S P S | E A R F U L S
C U T T H E M U S T A R D
E T T A | S O R T | B O I S E
D E L I | E L S E | L I N E R
E D E N | T E A S | E D G E R
```

52

```
D U D S | R A Y S | S K E E T
R H E O | O L E O | C L A S H
E U P H E M I S M | R E C T O
G R O O V E | M E T A P H O R
S A T | A R I | O P T
O N O M A T O P O E I A
J A M E S | P E O N Y | M A D
A W E D | T A T A S | R I T Z
V O W | S H I N S | P U R E E
A L L I T E R A T I O N
M O I | S N L | Q R S
O X Y M O R O N | S A M U E L
T E E U P | H Y P E R B O L E
I N A N E | N E S T | A T I P
C A R E D | O T I S | S E C T
```

53

```
T I E U P | C R A P S | R H O
I N T R O | L A U R A | H I P
F R O N T M O N K E Y | A K A
F I N | L A N D | I M P E L
J U N K B L O N D S
A B B A C Y | L E G I O N S
B L A C K | M U O N S | D I P
H A C K | T O K Y O | G I G I
O R K | B A S E D | D O Z E N
R E U T E R S | P E T E R S
P E T T Y C R A S H
H Y P E R | R U N E | A E C
A I L | A S S E T G R O W T H
W P A | Y E A S T | T O R R E
K E N | S A L T Y | S H Y E R
```

54

```
S P E W | F O O T | M A S S E
R O S A | A B L E | A L O O F
A L A R M D I D N T G O O F F
S O I S E E | S P A | E T A S
A M O S | I C E
C A R W O U L D N T S T A R T
E D O | S T A R | S A V O R
L I A R | S W O R D | R E D O
E E R I E | V I E W | R E M
B U S P A S S E D M Y S T O P
R O E | S E A T
B A A S | L A M | S T R A F E
O F F I C E W A S N T O P E N
M A R G O | A G U E | D E A D
B R O N X | Y I P S | E R R S
```

55

```
O B E Y S | T H A I | S C A D
C A P E K | H O L T | T R U E
T H E W I D E M I S S O U R I
O N E S P A D E | A I M S A T
I D A | A D E P T L Y
B O A S T S | U S E S
E A S E | I N F A T U A T E
T H I C K A S M O L A S S E S
A U N T E L L E R | M E M O
P L A T | I N C A P S
P H A N T O M | S S A
R E B U T S | E T A I L E R S
I N B R O A D D A Y L I G H T
A N O S | U N I T | E D G E D
M A T E | R A T E | D O S E S
```

56

```
F I R | C E S T A S | F A C T
A N E | A T C O S T | A L A R
W E H A V E A G O O D T I M E
C R I B | M A N N A | B I B
E R N E S T | E E N | A L L
T O G E T H E R | D A B B L E
T R E | L U L U S | R A E S
Y O G I B E R R A
O S S E | E L R O Y | S K I
T H E R A M | E V E N W H E N
T O T | M E A | G E R U N D
A R F | E L L E N | I S N O
W E R E N O T T O G E T H E R
A U E L | T H A T I S | E D S
S P E D | T O T A L S | D Y E
```

57

S	P	A	C	E		A	L	M	S		P	A	W	N
A	I	M	A	T		L	O	O	T		O	D	I	E
G	L	O	V	E	O	F	O	N	E	S	L	I	F	E
	E	S	E		F	A	N		V	A	I	N	E	R
			A	M	T		J	E	S	T				
	G	U	T	T	E	R	N	O	N	S	E	N	S	E
O	R	T		G	N	E	I	S	S		L	A	I	D
L	I	E	G	E		T	G	I		L	Y	I	N	G
E	E	R	O		S	A	H	A	R	A		V	E	E
G	R	O	O	M	W	I	T	H	A	V	I	E	W	
			D	U	E	L		I	S	M				
S	C	Y	L	L	A		H	O	T		P	A	S	
G	R	A	I	L	R	O	A	D	T	R	A	C	K	S
T	E	L	E		T	A	L	E		A	I	R	E	S
S	E	E	R		O	F	F	S		D	R	O	W	N

58

S	L	O	P	S		T	I	F	F		E	R	M	A
T	A	P	I	R		U	R	A	L		L	O	O	P
E	V	E	N	O	U	T	A	S	U	R	F	A	C	E
M	A	N	N		L	E	N	T		O	I	N	K	S
			A	O	N	E		G	I	N				
T	E	A	C	H	A	S	K	I	L	L		F	D	R
A	X	E	L	S		R	O	U	S	S	E	A	U	
H	A	R	E		G	R	O	U	T		U	R	N	S
O	M	I	S	S	I	O	N		E	N	A	C	T	
E	S	E		C	L	E	A	N	T	A	B	L	E	S
			A	R	T		I	S	T	O				
E	L	I	D	E		S	P	C	A		N	A	R	K
G	O	D	O	W	N	T	H	E	R	U	N	W	A	Y
G	L	O	B		B	A	I	L		P	E	R	I	L
Y	A	L	E		A	B	L	Y		S	T	Y	L	E

59

B	L	A	B		M	E	N	S	A		S	H	A	D
O	A	H	U		A	X	I	A	L		H	E	R	O
A	V	E	R		E	T	H	Y	L	M	E	R	T	Z
C	A	M	E	O		I	S	M	E		T	I	E	
			A	L	K	Y	L	S	E	L	T	Z	E	R
C	L	A	U	D	I	O		O	N	E	A			
A	E	C		I	N	K	Y		I	R	A	S		
M	E	R	C	E	D	E	S	B	E	N	Z	E	N	E
		P	R	E	Z		L	O	D	I		B	O	W
			A	B	B	A		T	I	N	C	A	N	S
F	E	R	R	O	U	S	W	H	E	E	L			
R	A	E		E	S	S	E		S	U	D	A	N	
E	S	T	E	R	B	U	N	N	Y		M	O	R	E
T	E	R	R		O	R	D	E	R		P	L	E	A
S	L	O	E		Y	E	S	E	S		S	L	A	T

60

E	D	I	C	T	S		W	A	R	N		R	A	T
R	U	N	O	U	T		A	L	O	E		E	L	I
R	E	C	O	N	A	R	T	I	S	T		T	E	N
			S	E	D	A	T	E	S		E	A	C	H
A	F	R		F	I	G	S		A	N	I	T	A	
B	E	E		U	A	W		S	A	N	D	L	O	T
B	A	G	E	L		E	T	E	R	N	A	L		
A	T	A	D		D	E	C	A	F		L	I	M	B
		L	I	N	E	D	U	P		A	L	G	E	R
S	I	F	T	E	R	S		O	S	U		H	A	I
P	O	R	E	D		A	W	E	S		T	N	T	
I	D	I	D		T	A	L	E	N	T	S			
R	I	D		R	E	M	O	R	S	E	C	O	D	E
E	N	A		O	L	I	N		E	R	O	D	E	S
D	E	Y		B	E	D	E		D	E	T	E	S	T

61

A	C	R	I	D		M	A	D	A	M		G	A	P
S	H	A	R	I		A	L	I	B	I		U	G	H
P	I	N	K	S	T	R	I	P	E	S		N	R	A
			T	A	C	T		L	A	K	E	S		
N	E	B	B	I	S	H		F	I	A	N	C	E	E
A	V	A	I	L	S		P	A	C	I	N	O		
V	I	R	A	L		J	A	D	E	D		N	B	A
E	L	K	S		C	O	V	E	S		S	T	U	B
S	S	T		P	O	K	E	D		W	O	R	D	Y
		E	A	R	N	E	D		B	E	F	O	G	S
M	A	N	L	I	E	R		B	O	T	T	L	E	S
A	D	D	L	E		G	I	R	L					
T	O	E		S	T	A	R	K	G	A	Z	I	N	G
E	R	R		T	E	P	E	E		N	O	O	N	E
Y	E	S		S	A	T	Y	R		D	O	N	E	E

62

C	A	S	T	E		C	R	A	M		C	O	K	E
O	F	T	E	N		H	U	L	A		E	V	E	R
G	R	A	T	E	F	U	L	D	E	A	D	E	Y	E
N	I	L	E		A	R	E	A		B	A	R	S	
A	C	E		B	I	N	D		B	U	R	S	T	S
C	A	R	E	E	R	S		H	O	T		H	O	P
			R	A	Y		W	E	B		T	O	N	Y
	P	E	A	R	L	J	A	M	B	O	R	E	E	
C	O	N	S		A	U	G		Y	O	U			
O	K	S		T	N	T		A	P	P	E	A	R	S
D	E	N	I	E	D		E	L	I	S		T	E	L
	W	A	V	E		A	N	O	N		U	R	S	A
A	E	R	O	S	M	I	T	H	S	O	N	I	A	N
L	E	E	R		I	D	E	A		A	D	U	L	T
E	D	D	Y		T	A	R	S		T	O	M	E	S

63

O	F	F	E	D		C	A	T		F	R	A	N	C
B	O	O	L	A		H	Q	S		R	O	L	E	O
J	E	R	K	Y		A	U	K		A	B	O	V	E
	B	O	L	D	F	A	S	H	I	O	N	E	D	
A	B	E		I	R	E		A	L	T	E	R	S	
B	E	A	G	L	E	S	C	O	U	T				
E	L	R	O	Y		H	A	L	Y	A	R	D	S	
E	L	E	E		A	L	I	F	S		B	O	R	A
T	A	R	R	A	G	O	N		B	O	R	I	S	
			B	R	O	A	D	H	O	U	S	E	S	
A	C	C	U	S	E		O	O	X		C	R	Y	
B	O	U	N	C	E	O	F	F	L	E	S	H		
E	A	R	T	O		O	O	F		D	I	A	M	S
A	T	E	I	N		Z	O	E		U	N	C	A	S
M	I	R	E	D		E	D	D		P	S	H	A	W

64

S	U	M	S		S	H	A	L	T		F	E	L	T
I	S	A	Y		C	O	R	E	A		O	P	I	E
G	U	L	L	F	R	O	M	I	P	A	N	E	M	A
N	A	T		O	A	K	S		E	N	D	E	A	R
S	L	A	L	O	M	S		A	S	T	A			
			E	L	S		A	R	T	E		H	A	Y
A	L	O	N	E		B	L	U	R		A	I	L	S
M	E	A	N	D	B	O	O	B	Y	M	C	G	E	E
M	A	R	Y		R	O	N	A		O	T	H	E	R
O	K	S		D	A	N	G		S	N	O			
			D	O	N	E		M	I	R	R	O	R	S
A	C	C	O	R	D		S	A	G	O		H	U	E
S	H	R	I	K	E	U	P	T	H	E	B	A	N	D
S	A	U	L		I	R	A	T	E		A	R	I	A
T	R	E	Y		S	I	R	E	D		M	A	N	N

189

65

```
E S P Y   A T T I C   M A L L
M E A D   R H I N O   A G E E
M A Y S   M E C C A   R I N G
A R C   D O R S A L   F I N N S
    Z A I R E     M A N G Y
S H E R R Y   P R I C E
L O C K E   M A I N E   E G O
O O H S   M I N C E   O X E N
P T S   F I L T H   S K I L L
    D U L L Y   C U R T S Y
  D E R E K     C H E A P
F A M I L Y T H A I S   O D D
O N C E   W O O D S   F L E A
A C E S   A D O R E   B E L L
M E E T   Y O K E L   I S L E
```

66

```
P A R K A S   S C H N O O K S
A S S E R T   P R E A D M I T
G I V E M E Y O U R M O N E Y
E S P N   R O T S   R I V E
      E E S   T I N
D O N T D O T H I S I M A
A V E R T S   A L P H A B E T
N E H I   P R Y   S E T H
A R R E S T E D   B U T A N E
    U S C O N G R E S S M A N
      I N N   O L E
R O A R   A W O L   S I Z E
O K G I V E M E M Y M O N E Y
C L I M A X E D   U M P I R E
S A N E N E S S   P E S T O S
```

67

```
E L B A   S A C S   S E P A L
C E I L   U C L A   T R A D E
H A L L   S T E R   E A S E D
O N L Y T H E F I N E S T
E T E   R I D S   O P E R A S
D O D G E     G U S   A V E
  E N D   T O G   O M I T
P A I N T E R S V A R N I S H
O N C E   A O K   T E E
E T A   C R Y   A S I D E
T I N H A T   A S E C   N E V
  W I T H O U T A T R A C E
B L A N C   B R A G   A J A R
S M I T H   E A V E   R A N T
A N T S Y   Y S E R   A M T S
```

68

```
W A G O N   M I G S   A F R O
E L O P E   A D I T   I L E X
A P O T H E C A R Y G R A N T
R A D   I N A H O L E   P T A
A C H E   T B O N E S   J A I
W I E L D   R E D S   A L L
I N A W E   E S E   D O C
G O R E S       A N K L E
  T S K   S A S   M I K E Y
E T E   P E L T   N O L T E
A I D   A R A B I A   N U L L
S A M   P O L E C A T   G O I
T R A D E M A R K H A R M O N
L A C E   O N T O   C H A S E
A S K S   S E A N   T O N E R
```

69

```
A R O M A   C E C I L   S P A
C A B A L   A S A R E S U L T
I C O U L D N T W A I T F O R
D E E R   E V E S   A I D A
    I D E A     H A L
S U C C E S S S O I W E N T
A L L E N   C A R E   I U M
P T A   A L I K E   G T O
S R S   P I A F   B A H T S
A H E A D W I T H O U T I T
    D Y E   H E R D
A G O G   M A A M   I N C A
J O N A T H A N W I N T E R S
A T T R I B U T E   B O R E S
R O O   S O L I D   C R O W N
```

70

```
C U B A   B I S H O P   A L P
O N E S   A R C A D E   R A H
N E A P   B A R B E R   C R Y
F A M I L Y Q U E S T   H A S
U T I C A   B A S   M I M I
S E N   M R S   S A T A N I C
E N G   P O O H   U R G E S
    T O W N Q U I R E
I D A H O   S K I N   D A D
D E F U N C T   E N O   E V A
E F F S   O H S   F A V O R
A L I   Q U A C K O F D A W N
M A X   U P L A N D   A L E E
E T E   A L I N E D   P U R R
N E S   L E A S E S   T E S S
```

71

```
S O D A   E V I L   S A B L E
P A Y S   V I V A   T Y L E R
A R E T H E S E S P A N I S H
  R U N E   S I R   G S A
O N I O N S   B O L D   H E R
R O B   G O Y A   L U S T E D
E L I S   A R I O S O
I D O N T K N O W T H E Y
  S E E S A W   O R A L
S C R A W L   R A S H   I R E
I L E   S L E D   H A V E N T
E E L   C O G   K I W I
S A I D A N Y T H I N G Y E T
T R E E S   P E A T   I O T A
A S S E T   T Y N E   L O C O
```

72

```
S T A R   P S S T   U P S E T
A R L O   S E N D   M A U V E
L O U D T H A I S   P I P E R
T I M E W A R P   M I N E R S
    N E W S   G A R   R Y E
B U T T E   A L D E R S
U N O   T O S S E D   N I N E
S T U B   R H I N O   A G E D
Y O G A   C L A N G S   H A G
    H Y P H E N   H A S T Y
A V G   R I P   S P O T
S O U S E D   O P E R E T T A
T W I N E   S N A K E E Y E S
R E S I N   A C R E   S N A P
O D E T S   T E E S   E E L S
```

73

```
COBS .RANDI. SALE
UVEA .OCEAN. TRIX
JELLYBEANS .ROTI
ONATOOT. STJAMES
.ALTOS. OPART..
AWINK. THAWS...
TOOTSIEROLL .ODD
OWN. OVINE. DUO
ZSA. SWEDISHFISH
..BLARE. OINKS.
OPERA. SHIMS...
CHEETAH ONESTEP
TORE. JUJYFRUITS
ENID. AGILE. REDS
TEES. ROGER. ERST
```

74

```
OPERA PALP .ANE
KARAT ALIE OPED
RUSTBUSTER NEVE
ALT ENTERS TMEN
.ISLE. OSIERS
STRATA CINEMA.
LOAM CHAN RESEW
ARI TEESOFF UTE
WELCH EENS ARON
.BREADS TAGEND
SPLAYS ROBO...
THAT SETUPS ART
RAZE AXASSESSOR
USER YAKS NIECE
MER SMEE TEASE
```

75

```
RUSSIAN ATLEAST
ABALONE GOINGTO
REDONDO LUNCHED
ARABIAN ORG AND
...BAN TWEED...
MAME TOO DRAWIN
OWAR EAST IRINA
RAYON TSE ENLAI
PROVO SPAR EDNA
HERETO ORE DEED
RANAT MAI...
ADO TEM CONFABS
CANDIDA ATTIMES
THEDOGS SEEDERS
ESSENES ASSORTS
```

76

```
BLEEP THERE VAN
MARSH RAWER EGO
WHATYOUHOPE LEO
...SLINK. SONS
UNITIES ASTUTE
TOBECOMEAFTER.
AREAS LITUP...
HAGS GOUDA OMAR
.PROUD ONICE.
YOURTEENFIRES
GLOOMY DEFTEST
LAWN TRIAD...
ATL YOUASPARENT
DIE DANNO YOYOS
END SKEIN SWEDE
```

77

```
TOYS HADON SPOT
AREA ALIBI YETI
SILL STAIN NEON
TELEPHONEJACKS.
ELEMI ASAN ACT
SSR ETA TABOO
.BROCCOLITOPS
OSLO READY MOES
GUYSANDDOLLS.
LINES REO ATA
ETC ASHE LIRAS
.CHOPPINGBLOCKS
MAIN APNEA WHEE
ISNT SPINS AIRS
LEGO MOSES NESS
```

78

```
ASST ABBA HARDY
SETH PLUS OPERA
INRE PORT URIAH
DOUBLECROSSING.
ORTEGA AEC
.SELLINGPOINT
AJET TALE ETNAS
SAS SORIGHT TIP
AGASP RARE POLS
PRIMARYCOLOR.
AND ISOBAR
SOCIALSECURITY
PICKA OTRO AGRA
UTTER LYNN THIN
GUARD AXES ETAS
```

79

```
ROPER JEAN OLLA
ARISE EYRE LOON
TARPS WECANDONO
ETA UPI STOPSIN
DOT LISP IRE
GREATTHINGSONLY
BSA GALE USE
ACHE PASTA SPUN
DOE BASK SEE
SMALLTHINGSWITH
DOO NOOK NEA
SARCASM DWI URN
GREATLOVE MORES
TEST AVIA OBESE
SATE PEEL SISAL
```

80

```
SWISS STOP KHAN
CINCH MONA ABRA
UPTHEPARTY BOIS
MELO ARCH COMET
OUTTHEBUBBLY
SVELTE RUBS.
LEVEE PHONE WEB
ATAD BREAK BATE
BON PLEAD FORTE
LIAR GANDER
INTOTHEHOUSE
NOWAY COTS ILSA
COIF FORTHEDOOR
ANNE ERSE FLARE
SEER EDER TENTS
```

81

```
JAWS  BRAT  HAWKS
EPIC  RUBE  ETHEL
FISH  ONAN  AMORE
FEELINGBAAD   ORD
    EDT  EMCEED
SAMPLER   TRAUMA
ELOPE  ESSO  UNIT
ELO  SPECTRA  ICE
PAVE  EDIE  MATRI
SHIRER   PLANSON
  ERMINE  ANT
DIS  BLACKMAAGIC
INTEL  ROWE  COMO
SCARE  CLAN  IRAN
HAREM  SENT  DECK
```

82

```
FRIDAY   BLACKCAT
DANUBE   REVEILLE
ANSELM   ANGELICA
   SUEDES    NOM
ITS  SNO  LEICAS
THETHIRTEENTH
TECH    ANTIC
YOYOS  UKE  DHABI
   ROONE   EXAM
 WALKINGUNDERA
COAXED   EPA  DEN
ALI   WASHUP
RIVERRAT   ISLAND
IVEGOTIT   LEELEE
BADOMENS   LADDER
```

83

```
EGAD  ADAM  RADAR
NARY  DORA  IMAGE
DICE  HUES  VELUM
 THREEBSSHEBEES
    ART   BRA
NATIVE  BROS  RAW
AMUSE  DEEM  SERA
BIBISFREEBIECBS
ONES  EARL  SETON
BOD  ANTS  ASSORT
    ARC   GNU
 SEABEESPHOEBES
LIMBO  WOOD  IDEA
AREAL  APSE  DDAY
TENSE  NETS  SYNE
```

84

```
SHOD   FILS   SCUM
PURR  ORNOT  TONY
EBAN  DUANE  ALVA
ACCORDINGTOPLAN
KAL  ESTES  CHARM
SPEED   HIE   PIA
  NBC  ROSA  SER
 ASGODINTENDED
ILO  WITS   EVA
LIP  TIS  ISLAM
LEROI  ADORE  ALA
INAPERFECTWORLD
CANE  CARTE  KIPS
ITON  ACMES  RARE
TESS  STAT  ATON
```

85

```
CALC  CLAM  GOPRO
ALIA  RANG  ALLAN
RANKLEDAMATEURS
BIGEASY   ROOMIE
   WIT  ADM  LENT
MOLARS   DIANE
OPAL  ASONE  PSI
BUCKLEDPRIVATES
SSE  ARIAS  LUNE
  ADHOC  POLITE
OPED  ASE  LPS
RAIDER   BEETRED
DUELEDFORARAISE
ELIEL  IRAS  ROAR
ROODS  GENE  STUN
```

86

```
SCRIP  SAMI  TOMB
PHONO  EBAN  IDEO
AESOP  CUTTHROAT
WANDERTHEEARTH
   EINE   RAN
 SAVETHEPLANET
UTICA  EROS   IRR
TACT  EDSEL  BCDE
ELK  GNUS  FAHEY
SCOURTHEGLOBE
   PER   RATE
CHANGETHEWORLD
LAKEGARDA  MUIRS
ALEX  TUTS  ATLAS
PERT  SEVE  THYME
```

87

```
QUEEG  SHAD  CRAB
ULTRA  TONE  HUME
INTER  ELEV  APIA
TAE  BAREWITNESS
   TARN  LATEST
FAREGROUNDS
LOIRE   TOOKBACK
INNS  SWING  ALAI
PEDESTAL   ASTIN
 HARERAISING
ASKFOR   ACRO
STAREMASTER  WBA
TOPE  ALOE  AAHED
ROUT  POND  IRINA
OPTS  STYX  DIZZY
```

88

```
ASIF  NOME  BITTE
RENE  AHEM  ENRON
MERV  VINE  MUONS
 KEEPYOURWORDS
   RAMA  IRAE
 SOFTANDTENDER
CAREEN  RUNS  BOO
BLOW  PIS  SOOT
SEN  NELL  PSALMS
 SOMEDAYYOUMAY
   OMIT  ERIE
 HAVETOEATTHEM
JULES  OLGA  EXAM
RADII  NOEL  RELO
SCOTS  SIRS  ECTO
```